CALIFORNIA TEST PREP

Common Core Quiz Book

SBAC Mathematics

Grade 3

ISBN 978-1726095242

TEST MASTER PRESS

www.testmasterpress.com

CONTENTS

INTRODUCTION
For Parents, Teachers, and Tutors

About the Common Core State Standards

The state of California has adopted the Common Core State Standards. These standards describe the skills that students are expected to have. Student learning is based on these standards throughout the year, and all the questions on the state tests assess these standards. This quiz book covers all the skills listed in the Common Core State Standards.

Completing the Quizzes

The quizzes are divided into the main areas, or domains, of the Common Core State Standards. There is one quiz for each specific skill that students need. For each quiz, the difficulty of questions increases from simple to complex. Many quizzes also include guided questions that will help students understand what is expected in answers.

About the Smarter Balanced Assessments

Students in California are assessed each school year by taking the Smarter Balanced, or the SBAC, assessments. These assessments include a range of question types, including performance tasks. This book will develop all the skills that students need for the assessment, while preparing students for the types of tasks they will need to complete.

Preparing for the Smarter Balanced Assessments

The Smarter Balanced (SBAC) assessments have key features that differ from previous tests. These features are described below.

- The tests are more rigorous and require a deeper understanding of math concepts.
- The tests have a wider range of question types. There are more constructed-response questions, more multi-step problems, and more questions involving advanced tasks.
- There are more questions that require students to explain mathematical concepts, show or explain their work, or justify answers.
- The tests are taken online and include computer-based questions. These involve tasks like ordering numbers, selecting points on a number line or graph, sorting items, completing number sentences and equations, and using fraction models.

This quiz book will prepare students for these key features. The questions have a wide range of formats, including questions that mimic the computer-based formats. The questions are more rigorous and include more advanced tasks. The skills assessed match the SBAC tests, with a greater focus on applying skills and on demonstrating in-depth understanding. By completing all the quizzes, students will develop a thorough understanding of the math skills required, and be prepared for all the types of tasks found on the SBAC assessments.

Quizzes 1 to 12

Operations and Algebraic Thinking

Directions

Read each question carefully. For each multiple-choice question, fill in the circle for the correct answer. For other types of questions, follow the directions given in the question.

You may use a ruler to help you answer questions. You should answer the questions without using a calculator.

COMMON CORE SKILLS LIST
For Parents, Teachers, and Tutors

Quizzes 1 through 12 cover these skills from the Common Core State Standards.

Operations and Algebraic Thinking

Represent and solve problems involving multiplication and division.
1. Interpret products of whole numbers, e.g., interpret 5 × 7 as the total number of objects in 5 groups of 7 objects each.
2. Interpret whole-number quotients of whole numbers, e.g., interpret 56 ÷ 8 as the number of objects in each share when 56 objects are partitioned equally into 8 shares, or as a number of shares when 56 objects are partitioned into equal shares of 8 objects each.
3. Use multiplication and division within 100 to solve word problems in situations involving equal groups, arrays, and measurement quantities.
4. Determine the unknown whole number in a multiplication or division equation relating three whole numbers.

Understand properties of multiplication and the relationship between multiplication and division.
5. Apply properties of operations as strategies to multiply and divide.
6. Understand division as an unknown-factor problem.

Multiply and divide within 100.
7. Fluently multiply and divide within 100, using strategies such as the relationship between multiplication and division or properties of operations. By the end of Grade 3, know from memory all products of two one-digit numbers.

Solve problems involving the four operations, and identify and explain patterns in arithmetic.
8. Solve two-step word problems using the four operations. Represent these problems using equations with a letter standing for the unknown quantity. Assess the reasonableness of answers using mental computation and estimation strategies including rounding.
9. Identify arithmetic patterns (including patterns in the addition table or multiplication table), and explain them using properties of operations.

Quiz 1: Understanding Multiplication

1   Which expression is represented by the model below?

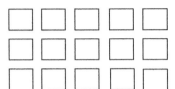

    Ⓐ 3 × 3   Ⓑ 3 × 15   Ⓒ 5 × 3   Ⓓ 10 × 2

2   A classroom has the student desks organized as shown below.

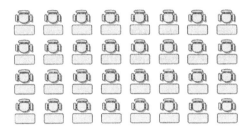

    Which expression shows how to find the number of student desks?

    Ⓐ 4 × 4   Ⓑ 8 × 2   Ⓒ 8 × 8   Ⓓ 8 × 4

3   Sierra organizes 40 coins into equal rows. Which of these could describe the rows? Select all the possible answers.

    ☐ 20 rows of 20 coins each

    ☐ 8 rows of 5 coins each

    ☐ 40 rows of 10 coins each

    ☐ 4 rows of 4 coins each

    ☐ 6 rows of 7 coins each

    ☐ 10 rows of 4 coins each

4   Rebecca buys 8 packets of pencils. There are 8 pencils in each packet. How many pencils does she buy in all? Write your answer on the line below.

Answer _____ pencils

5   Write and solve a multiplication expression to answer each question.

Sam plants 6 rows of 5 flowers each. How many flowers did he plant?

_____ × _____ = _____

There are 9 piles of 3 books each. How many books are there in all?

_____ × _____ = _____

Tai folds 8 napkins each minute. How many can he fold in 10 minutes?

_____ × _____ = _____

Donnie buys 6 tickets for $7 each. How many dollars does he spend in all?

_____ × _____ = _____

There are 8 potatoes in each bag. How many potatoes are in 5 bags?

_____ × _____ = _____

6   There are 48 students at a music camp. They need to be divided into groups with an equal number of students in each group. Complete the table to describe four different ways the students could be divided.

Number of Groups	Number of Students in Each Group

7   Jessica was asked to write a description of a situation where the total number of items is represented by the expression below.

7×24

Jessica started her description, as shown below. Complete the description.

There were 7 boxes of water on a truck. _____

_____

_____

8   Davis has 3 basketball lessons a week. Write a description of a problem Davis could solve with the expression below.

3×60

_____

_____

_____

9   A store sells notepads for $3 each. Write a description of a problem that could be solved with the expression below.

3×15

_____

_____

_____

10 Avril uses 6 beads to make a bracelet, as shown below.

Complete the table to show the number of beads needed to make each number of bracelets.

Number of Bracelets	Expression	Total Number of Beads
1	1×6	6
2		
3		
4		
5		

11 In the space below, draw one way 16 coins can be organized into equal rows. Then complete the equation to show the total number of coins.

Equation _____ × _____ = _____

12 Otis buys 3 sheets of stickers. Each sheet has 6 rows of 4 stickers each. Write an equation to find the total number of stickers. Then write the number of stickers on the blank line.

Equation

Answer _____ stickers

Quiz 2: Understanding Division

1   Which equation is represented by the model below?

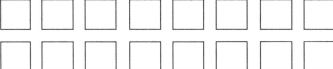

Ⓐ 24 ÷ 8 = 3   Ⓑ 8 ÷ 4 = 2   Ⓒ 21 ÷ 7 = 3   Ⓓ 72 ÷ 3 = 24

2   There are 12 sunflowers in a bunch.

The sunflowers are divided evenly between 3 vases. Which equation can be used to find how many sunflowers are in each vase?

Ⓐ 12 ÷ 6 = 2   Ⓑ 12 × 3 = 36   Ⓒ 12 ÷ 3 = 4   Ⓓ 36 ÷ 3 = 12

3   Select all the situations that can be represented by 30 ÷ 3.

☐ A teacher sorts 30 students into 3 equal groups.

☐ A class of 30 students gets 3 new students.

☐ A classroom has 30 desks organized into 3 equal rows.

☐ A group of 30 students give a talk for 3 minutes each.

☐ A test has 30 questions worth 3 points each.

☐ A classroom with 30 desks has 3 empty desks.

☐ There are 3 school buses and 30 students on each bus.

4   Write and solve a division expression to answer each question.

Mia sorts 30 blocks into 6 equal piles. How many blocks are in each pile?

_____ ÷ _____ = _____

A coach puts 28 boys in 4 equal teams. How many boys are in each team?

_____ ÷ _____ = _____

Joel earns $9 per hour. How many hours does he work to make $72?

_____ ÷ _____ = _____

Muffins sell for $4 each. How many muffins need to be sold to make $32?

_____ ÷ _____ = _____

5   Mr. Denton is ordering pizzas for a party. Each pizza has 8 slices.

Complete the equation to show how to find the number of pizzas he will need to order to have 40 slices.

_____ ÷ _____ = _____

6   Hal has 80 photos. He places them in equal groups and has no photos left over. Circle the three other numbers below that could be the number of groups he sorted the photos into.

②   3   4   5   6   7   8   9

Write numbers on the lines to find the number of photos in each group.

80 ÷ _2_ = _40_   80 ÷ ____ = ____

80 ÷ ____ = ____   80 ÷ ____ = ____

7   Carrie was asked to write a description of a situation where the number of items is represented by the expression below.

   24 ÷ 6

Carrie started her description, as shown below. Complete the description.

There are 24 students in a class. _____

_____

_____

8   Morgan has 36 baseball cards. Write a description of a problem Morgan could solve with the expression below.

   36 ÷ 4

_____

_____

_____

9   Anna has 50 candies in a bag. Write a description of a problem Anna could solve with the expression below.

   50 ÷ 10

_____

_____

_____

10   Leon has 20 apples. Draw circles around the apples to place them in 5 equal groups.

How many apples are in each group? _____ apples

11   Lenny has 12 quarters. He sorts them into groups of 4. Draw a diagram to show how many groups of quarters he will have. Then complete the equation to show how to find how many groups he will have.

Equation _____ ÷ _____ = _____

12   Marina has 18 tomatoes and 3 bags. She places an equal number of tomatoes in each bag.

Write an equation to show how many tomatoes she places in each bag. Then write the number of tomatoes in each bag on the blank line.

Equation

Answer _____ tomatoes

Quiz 3: Using Multiplication to Solve Problems

1   Juan and Lisa have the same number of dimes. Juan sorted his dimes into 6 piles with 5 dimes in each pile. Lisa sorted her dimes into 3 equal piles. How many dimes were in each of Lisa's piles?

Ⓐ 9   Ⓑ 10   Ⓒ 15   Ⓓ 30

2   Mrs. Donovan worked for 8 hours a day for 4 days of the week. She earned $10 for each hour she worked. How much did Mrs. Donovan earn in all?

Ⓐ $80   Ⓑ $120   Ⓒ $320   Ⓓ $400

3   A stores sells small milkshakes for $2 each, medium milkshakes for $3 each, and large milkshakes for $5 each. Write 1, 2, 3, and 4 on the lines to place the orders from lowest cost to highest cost.

_____ 4 small milkshakes and 2 medium milkshakes

_____ 3 large milkshakes

_____ 2 small milkshakes and 3 medium milkshakes

_____ 4 medium milkshakes

4   Zac is organizing 36 chairs for a school play. Which of these are ways he could place all 36 chairs? Select all the possible answers.

☐ 4 rows of 9 chairs

☐ 5 rows of 7 chairs

☐ 8 rows of 4 chairs

☐ 6 rows of 6 chairs

☐ 3 rows of 10 chairs

☐ 6 rows of 3 chairs

5   Flour is sold in bags of 4 pounds each. A diner orders several bags of flour. Which of these could be the total number of pounds of flour? Circle all the possible answers.

20   26   30   36   42   44   52

How many pounds of flour would be in an order of 10 bags? _____ pounds

6   The diagram below shows how tables and chairs are set up to seat all the guests at a wedding.

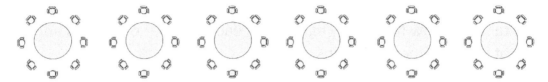

Complete the sentence to describe how the tables are set up.

There are _____ tables and each table seats _____ people.

How many people can be seated at the wedding?

Show your work.

Answer _____ people

The wedding planner decides there should be only 6 people at each table. How many tables would be needed to seat all the people?

Show your work.

Answer _____ tables

7   The list shows how long four team members practice baseball each week.

Milton practices for 20 minutes 7 times a week.
Rod practices for 30 minutes 5 times a week.
Paolo practices for 60 minutes 2 times a week.
Trey practices for 50 minutes 4 times a week.

Which team member practices for the least amount of time? _____

Which team member practices for the most amount of time? _____

8   Eggs are sold in cartons of 6 eggs each. Each carton costs $3. Complete the table to show how many eggs are in each number of cartons and the cost of each number of cartons.

Number of Cartons of Eggs	Total Number of Eggs	Total Cost (in dollars)
4		
6		
8		
10		

9   Hailey plants 3 rows of roses with 8 roses in each row. How many roses does she plant in all? Write your answer below.

Answer _____ roses

10   Lester buys 6 tickets to a play for $7 each. What is the total cost of the tickets? Write your answer below.

Answer $_____

11   Stefan made a path by laying down planks of wood, as shown below.

How many planks of wood did he use?

Show your work.

Answer _____ planks of wood

Each plank of wood was 4 feet long. How long was the path?

Show your work.

Answer _____ feet

12   Rex is planting lettuces in his garden. He has 28 lettuces to plant. He plants the lettuces in 6 rows with an equal number of lettuces in each row. What is the most number of lettuces he can plant in each of the 6 rows? Use words or pictures to show how you found your answer.

Answer _____ lettuces

Quiz 4: Using Division to Solve Problems

1   Li put 54 pens into 9 equal groups. How many pens were in each group?

      Ⓐ 5   Ⓑ 6   Ⓒ 7   Ⓓ 8

2   A farmer packed 72 bottles of orange juice into packs of 8 bottles each. How many packs were there?

      Ⓐ 6   Ⓑ 7   Ⓒ 8   Ⓓ 9

3   Which of these would have 4 students in each team? Select all the correct answers.

    ☐ 28 students divided into 7 equal teams

    ☐ 36 students divided into 6 equal teams

    ☐ 40 students divided into 8 equal teams

    ☐ 24 students divided into 6 equal teams

    ☐ 32 students divided into 8 equal teams

    ☐ 44 students divided into 4 equal teams

4   A baker had 80 pounds of flour. He placed equal amounts into bags. He filled 10 bags. How many pounds were in each bag?

    Answer _____ pounds

5   A pet store has 48 fish. They want to put 4 fish in each fish tank. How many fish tanks would be needed?

    Answer _____ fish tanks

6   Students at a bake sale divided cakes into 8 pieces and sold each piece for $2. If the total sales were $80, how many complete cakes did they sell?

Show your work.

Answer _____ cakes

7   Jay bought 8 pens for $3 each. Leanne bought 6 notebooks. The price of each notebook was the same. Leanne spent the same total amount as Jay.

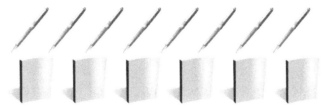

How much was each notebook?

Show your work.

Answer $_____

8   Mr. Anderson bought 12 children's ticket to a show for $4 each. Mrs. Chavez bought 8 adult tickets for the same total amount. How much was each adult ticket?

Show your work.

Answer $_____

9 Four classes at a school all have the desks arranged in equal rows. The table shows how the desks are arranged in each class. Complete the missing numbers in the table.

Class	Total Number of Desks	Number of Rows of Desks	Number of Desks in each Row
Mrs. Jenson	30	5	
Mr. Hoy	28		7
Miss Parker		4	8
Mr. Lewis	27		9

10 The table below shows how many cups of juice are filled for different numbers of cartons of juice.

Cartons of Juice	Cups of Juice
3	12
5	20
6	?
?	28
?	32
9	36

How many cups of juice are filled from 6 cartons of juice? _____ cups

How many cartons of juice will be needed to serve 28 cups? _____ cartons

How many cartons of juice will be needed to serve 32 cups? _____ cartons

Cups of juice are sold for $2 each. How many cups of juice need to be sold to make $80? _____ cups

11   Al made the diagram below to show how he will stack cans in equal rows.

Complete the equation and sentence to tell how all the cans are stacked.

_____ ÷ _____ = _____   There are _____ cans in _____ rows of _____ cans each.

Complete the equation to represent how the cans could be stacked in 3 rows. Then complete the sentence.

_____ ÷ _____ = _____   There are _____ cans in 3 rows of _____ cans each.

12   Students are making shapes by placing square tiles on a board. Tori used 64 tiles, Amelia used 54 tiles, Dina used 49 tiles, and Ivy used 50 tiles.

Who could have made a rectangle that was 5 tiles long? How many tiles high would the shape be? Show or explain how you found your answer.

Student _____   **Height** _____ tiles

Who could have made a rectangle that was 9 tiles long? How many tiles high would the shape be? Show or explain how you found your answer.

Student _____   **Height** _____ tiles

Which two students could have made square shapes? Show or explain how you found your answer.

Students _____ and _____

Quiz 5: Using Properties of Numbers

1   Which number sentence can be used to find the value of $63 \div 9$?

    Ⓐ $9 \times$ ___ $= 63$ Ⓑ $9 +$ ___ $= 63$ Ⓒ $9 \times 63 =$ ___   Ⓓ $9 + 63 =$ ___

2   Which number sentence can be used to check the value of $7 \times 3 = 21$?

    Ⓐ $21 \div 7 =$ ___   Ⓑ $21 + 7 =$ ___   Ⓒ $21 \times 3 =$ ___   Ⓓ $21 - 7 =$ ___

3   For each multiplication equation, complete two division equations that could be used to check the answer.

    $6 \times 4 = 24$ ____ $\div$ ____ $=$ ____   ____ $\div$ ____ $=$ ____

    $7 \times 6 = 42$ ____ $\div$ ____ $=$ ____   ____ $\div$ ____ $=$ ____

    $3 \times 9 = 27$ ____ $\div$ ____ $=$ ____   ____ $\div$ ____ $=$ ____

    $8 \times 4 = 32$ ____ $\div$ ____ $=$ ____   ____ $\div$ ____ $=$ ____

    $5 \times 7 = 35$ ____ $\div$ ____ $=$ ____   ____ $\div$ ____ $=$ ____

    $9 \times 8 = 72$ ____ $\div$ ____ $=$ ____   ____ $\div$ ____ $=$ ____

4   For each division equation, complete two multiplication equations that could be used to check the answer.

    $36 \div 4 = 9$ ____ $\times$ ____ $=$ ____   ____ $\times$ ____ $=$ ____

    $20 \div 4 = 5$ ____ $\times$ ____ $=$ ____   ____ $\times$ ____ $=$ ____

    $18 \div 2 = 9$ ____ $\times$ ____ $=$ ____   ____ $\times$ ____ $=$ ____

    $48 \div 8 = 6$ ____ $\times$ ____ $=$ ____   ____ $\times$ ____ $=$ ____

    $30 \div 6 = 5$ ____ $\times$ ____ $=$ ____   ____ $\times$ ____ $=$ ____

    $28 \div 4 = 7$ ____ $\times$ ____ $=$ ____   ____ $\times$ ____ $=$ ____

5   Complete the missing values in the equations below.

$4 \times 6 = \underline{\hspace{1cm}} \times 4$ $7 \times 1 = \underline{\hspace{1cm}} \times 7$ $5 \times \underline{\hspace{1cm}} = 6 \times 5$

$8 \times 9 = \underline{\hspace{1cm}} \times 8$ $5 \times 4 = \underline{\hspace{1cm}} \times 5$ $2 \times \underline{\hspace{1cm}} = 8 \times 2$

$3 \times 5 = \underline{\hspace{1cm}} \times 3$ $9 \times 3 = \underline{\hspace{1cm}} \times 9$ $1 \times \underline{\hspace{1cm}} = 7 \times 1$

6   Complete the table to show the two steps in finding the value of each expression. The first one has been completed for you.

Expression	Step 1	Step 2
$(3 \times 4) \times 10$	12×10	120
$(3 \times 2) \times 8$		
$(2 \times 4) \times 9$		
$(14 \div 7) \times 6$		
$(36 \div 6) \times 4$		
$(45 \div 5) \times 7$		

7   Complete the missing values to create an equivalent expression. Then find the value of the expression.

$4 \times (6 + 2) = (\underline{\hspace{1cm}} \times \underline{\hspace{1cm}}) + (\underline{\hspace{1cm}} \times \underline{\hspace{1cm}})$

Answer _____

8   Select all the expressions that are equal to 81.

☐ $9 \times (4 + 5)$ ☐ $(9 \times 3) + (9 \times 6)$

☐ $(8 + 1) \times 7$ ☐ $(5 \times 4) + (6 \times 3)$

☐ $3 \times 6 \times 9$ ☐ $(1 \times 9) + (9 \times 9)$

9   Which of these shows a correct way to find $60 \div 2 \div 6$?

Ⓐ $60 \div (6 - 2) = 60 \div 4 = 15$ Ⓑ $60 \div 2 = 30,\ 30 \times 6 = 180$

Ⓒ $60 \div 6 = 10,\ 10 \div 2 = 5$ Ⓓ $(60 - 6) \div 2 = 54 \div 2 = 27$

10   Complete the number sentences by writing the missing number in each blank space. Then complete the calculation.

$14 \times 2 = (10 \times 2) + (\underline{\quad} \times 2)$ $18 \times 4 = (10 \times 4) + (\underline{\quad} \times 4)$

$= \underline{\qquad} + \underline{\qquad}$ $= \underline{\qquad} + \underline{\qquad}$

$= \underline{\qquad}$ $= \underline{\qquad}$

$25 \times 6 = (20 \times 6) + (5 \times \underline{\quad})$ $36 \times 3 = (30 \times 3) + (6 \times \underline{\quad})$

$= \underline{\qquad} + \underline{\qquad}$ $= \underline{\qquad} + \underline{\qquad}$

$= \underline{\qquad}$ $= \underline{\qquad}$

$15 \times 3 = (\underline{\quad} \times 3) + (\underline{\quad} \times 3)$ $43 \times 5 = (\underline{\quad} \times 5) + (\underline{\quad} \times 5)$

$= \underline{\qquad} + \underline{\qquad}$ $= \underline{\qquad} + \underline{\qquad}$

$= \underline{\qquad}$ $= \underline{\qquad}$

$28 \times 7 = (\underline{\quad} \times \underline{\quad}) + (\underline{\quad} \times \underline{\quad})$ $52 \times 7 = (\underline{\quad} \times \underline{\quad}) + (\underline{\quad} \times \underline{\quad})$

$= \underline{\qquad} + \underline{\qquad}$ $= \underline{\qquad} + \underline{\qquad}$

$= \underline{\qquad}$ $= \underline{\qquad}$

11   Complete the number sentences below to show three different ways to complete the calculation in two steps.

$$2 \times 5 \times 6$$

_____ × _____ = 10, then _____ × _____ = _____

_____ × _____ = 12, then _____ × _____ = _____

_____ × _____ = 30, then _____ × _____ = _____

12   Coins are placed in 2 rows of 16 coins each. Greg divided the coins into two groups to calculate the total number of coins, as shown below.

Complete the expression to show how to find how many coins there are. Write the answer on the line.

(2 × _____) + (2 × _____)

Answer _____ coins

Draw rectangles to divide the coins into two equal groups. Then complete the expression to show how to find how many coins there are. Write the answer on the line.

(_____ × _____) + (_____ × _____)

Answer _____ coins

Quiz 6: Using Multiplication and Division Equations

1 Carter organized 36 apples into 4 equal piles. Which number sentence could be used to find the number of apples in each pile?

Ⓐ 4 ÷ ___ = 36   Ⓑ 4 × ___ = 36

Ⓒ 36 × 4 = ___   Ⓓ ___ ÷ 4 = 36

2 Each milk carton below contains 8 fluid ounces of milk.

Which number sentence could be used to find how many fluid ounces of milk there are in all?

Ⓐ 4 ÷ ___ = 8   Ⓑ 4 × ___ = 8

Ⓒ 8 × 4 = ___   Ⓓ 8 ÷ ___ = 4

3 Mr. Baxter earns $9 for each hour he works. He earned $72 for one day's work. Which number sentences could be used to find how many hours he worked that day? Select all the correct answers.

☐ 72 ÷ ___ = 9   ☐ 72 ÷ 9 = ___

☐ 9 × ___ = 72   ☐ ___ × 9 = 72

☐ 9 ÷ ___ = 72   ☐ 9 × 72 = ___

4 Maria sold 8 cupcakes for an equal amount and made a total of $24. Which of these describes how much she sold each cupcake for?

Ⓐ $3 each, because 24 ÷ 8 = 3

Ⓑ $16 each, because 24 - 8 = 16

Ⓒ $32 each, because 24 + 8 = 32

Ⓓ $192 each, because 24 × 8 = 192

5   Write an equation to match each statement. Then find the missing number.
The first one has been completed for you.

Statement	Equation	Missing Number
3 times a number is equal to 18	3 × ___ = 18	6
30 divided by a number is equal to 10		
a number times 6 is equal to 42		
twice a number is equal to 12		
a number divided by 5 is equal to 7		

6   Write multiplication expressions to complete the list of all the factors pairs for each number.

Number	Factor Pairs

Number	Factor Pairs			
12	1 × 12	____ x ____	____ x ____	
16	1 × 16	____ x ____	____ x ____	
18	1 × 18	____ x ____	____ x ____	
20	1 × 20	____ x ____	____ x ____	
24	1 × 24	____ x ____	____ x ____	____ x ____
30	1 × 30	____ x ____	____ x ____	____ x ____
40	1 × 40	____ x ____	____ x ____	____ x ____

7   Darren had 56 photos to place in an album. He placed 8 photos on each page. Complete the equation to show how to find the number of pages of the album Darren filled. Then write the answer below.

56 ÷ _____ = _____

Answer _____ pages

Darren wants to add 4 star stickers to each page with photos on it. Complete the equation to find how many star stickers Darren will need. Then write the answer below.

_____ × 4 = _____

Answer _____ stickers

8   Lila baked 72 muffins for a bake sale. She packed them into bags of 8 muffins each. Complete the equation to show how to find how many bags of muffins Lila had. Then write the answer below.

_____ ÷ _____ = _____

Answer _____ bags

Lila sold the bags of muffins for $4 each and sold all the bags. Complete the equation to show how much Lila made, in dollars. Then write the answer below.

_____ × _____ = _____

Answer $_____

9   Becca is organizing tables for a party. She has 28 people to seat and she wants to seat 4 people at each table. Write an equation to show how to find the number of tables that Becca will need. Then write the answer below.

Answer _____ tables

Becca wants to put a vase of flowers on each table, with 3 sunflowers in each vase. Write an equation to show how to find the number of sunflowers needed. Then write the answer below.

Answer _____ sunflowers

10   Mr. Palmer is organizing students into groups to complete a science project. He puts 27 students into groups of 3 students each. Write an equation to show how to find the number of groups. Then write the answer below.

Answer _____ groups

Each group of students is given 5 leaves. Write an equation to show how to find the number of leaves in all. Then write the answer below.

Answer _____ leaves

Quiz 7: Using Multiplication Facts

1   What is the value of the expression 6 × 4?

  Ⓐ 18   Ⓑ 24   Ⓒ 28   Ⓓ 32

2   Joe says that if he runs 5 miles twice a week, he will run a total of 7 miles. Which of these describes Joe's statement?

  Ⓐ He is correct because the sum of 5 and 2 is 7.

  Ⓑ He is correct because 7 is 2 more than 5.

  Ⓒ He is incorrect because the product of 5 and 2 is 10.

  Ⓓ He is incorrect because 7 times 5 is equal to 35.

3   Which of these could be used to find the number of muffins that can be baked in the muffin tin below?

  Ⓐ the product of 3 and 4

  Ⓑ the product of 4 and 6

  Ⓒ the product of 6 and 6

  Ⓓ the product of 12 and 12

4   Select all the equations that are correct when the number 6 is placed on the blank line.

  ☐ 36 ÷ ___ = 4   ☐ 10 × ___ = 60

  ☐ 42 ÷ ___ = 7   ☐ 30 × 5 = ___

  ☐ 48 ÷ 8 = ___   ☐ ___ × 9 = 52

5 Complete each number sentence by writing the missing number on the blank line.

$7 \times 3 =$ _____ $3 \times 3 =$ _____ $1 \times 4 =$ _____

$6 \times 4 =$ _____ $5 \times 6 =$ _____ $8 \times 5 =$ _____

$2 \times 8 =$ _____ $8 \times 7 =$ _____ $3 \times 8 =$ _____

$9 \times 9 =$ _____ $6 \times 7 =$ _____ $7 \times 5 =$ _____

$4 \times 7 =$ _____ $9 \times 4 =$ _____ $2 \times 6 =$ _____

6 Complete each number sentence by writing the missing number on the blank line.

$2 \times$ _____ $= 18$ $4 \times$ _____ $= 24$ $7 \times$ _____ $= 70$

_____ $\times 7 = 21$ _____ $\times 8 = 40$ _____ $\times 6 = 36$

$4 \times$ _____ $= 36$ $9 \times$ _____ $= 9$ $7 \times$ _____ $= 56$

_____ $\times 5 = 50$ _____ $\times 6 = 48$ _____ $\times 4 = 20$

7 Complete each number sentence by writing the missing 1-digit numbers on the blank lines.

____ $\times$ ____ $= 14$ ____ $\times$ ____ $= 35$ ____ $\times$ ____ $= 64$

____ $\times$ ____ $= 27$ ____ $\times$ ____ $= 48$ ____ $\times$ ____ $= 54$

____ $\times$ ____ $= 32$ ____ $\times$ ____ $= 63$ ____ $\times$ ____ $= 25$

8   Find the value of the missing number in each statement. Write the correct number on the blank line. Then write a division equation to show that the number is correct. The first one has been completed for you.

6 equals __24__ divided by 4 $24 \div 4 = 6$

8 equals ____ divided by 2   ____ ÷ ____ = ____

7 equals ____ divided by 9   ____ ÷ ____ = ____

5 equals ____ divided by 4   ____ ÷ ____ = ____

9 equals ____ divided by 3   ____ ÷ ____ = ____

9   Sawyer sells some baseball cards for $3 each. Which of these could be the total amount he makes?

Ⓐ $14   Ⓑ $15   Ⓒ $16   Ⓓ $17

10 Kelly makes a tower by placing layers of blocks on top of each other. Each layer has 4 blocks, as shown below.

Which of these could be the total number of blocks in Kelly's tower? Circle all the possible answers.

14   18   20   22   24   26   28   30   32   34

Explain why the numbers you did not circle are not possible answers.

_____

_____

_____

Quiz 8: Using Division Facts

1 What is the value of the expression 63 ÷ 9?

Ⓐ 6   Ⓑ 7   Ⓒ 8   Ⓓ 9

2 Jeremy says that if he places 12 coins in rows of 4, there will be 8 rows. Which of these describes Jeremy's statement?

Ⓐ He is correct because 4 less than 12 is equal to 8.

Ⓑ He is correct because the sum of 8 and 4 is 12.

Ⓒ He is incorrect because the product of 12 and 4 is 48.

Ⓓ He is incorrect because 12 divided by 4 is equal to 3.

3 Which of these describes a situation where there will be 6 students in each group?

Ⓐ 48 students divided into 8 equal groups

Ⓑ 56 students divided into 7 equal groups

Ⓒ 63 students divided into 7 equal groups

Ⓓ 72 students divided into 8 equal groups

4 Select all the equations that are correct when the number 3 is placed on the blank line.

☐ 25 ÷ ___ = 5   ☐ 10 × ___ = 30

☐ 18 ÷ ___ = 9   ☐ 8 × 5 = ___

☐ 21 ÷ ___ = 7   ☐ ___ × 4 = 24

☐ 3 ÷ 1 = ___   ☐ ___ × 9 = 27

☐ 15 ÷ 5 = ___   ☐ 7 × ___ = 42

5 Anna sorted 48 candies into equal groups, with none left over. Which of these could be the number of groups? Circle all the possible answers.

5   6   7   8   9   10

6 Complete each number sentence by writing the missing number on the blank line.

$12 \div 2 =$ _____ $63 \div 9 =$ _____ $25 \div 5 =$ _____

$24 \div 3 =$ _____ $56 \div 8 =$ _____ $18 \div 6 =$ _____

$35 \div 5 =$ _____ $60 \div 6 =$ _____ $36 \div 4 =$ _____

$70 \div 7 =$ _____ $9 \div 1 =$ _____ $49 \div 7 =$ _____

$36 \div 6 =$ _____ $32 \div 4 =$ _____ $72 \div 8 =$ _____

7 Complete each number sentence by writing the missing number on the blank line.

$8 \div$ _____ $= 2$ $27 \div$ _____ $= 9$ $16 \div$ _____ $= 4$

$20 \div$ _____ $= 5$ $90 \div$ _____ $= 10$ $18 \div$ _____ $= 2$

$54 \div$ _____ $= 6$ $42 \div$ _____ $= 7$ $64 \div$ _____ $= 8$

8 Complete each number sentence by writing the missing number on the blank line.

_____ $\div 7 = 3$ _____ $\div 2 = 8$ _____ $\div 5 = 8$

_____ $\div 6 = 5$ _____ $\div 9 = 5$ _____ $\div 8 = 6$

_____ $\div 3 = 10$ _____ $\div 1 = 4$ _____ $\div 9 = 9$

9   Find the value of the missing number in each statement. Write the correct number on the blank line. Then write a multiplication equation to show that the number is correct. The first one has been completed for you.

35 equals __5__ multiplied by 7 $5 \times 7 = 35$

64 equals _____ multiplied by 8   _____ × _____ = _____

36 equals _____ multiplied by 4   _____ × _____ = _____

14 equals _____ multiplied by 2   _____ × _____ = _____

48 equals _____ multiplied by 6   _____ × _____ = _____

10   Complete the table by writing a division equation that shows that the number is a factor. The first one has been completed for you.

Number	Factor	Equation
40	5	$40 \div 8 = 5$
32	8	
70	10	
18	6	
56	7	
27	3	

11   A coach wants to divide 30 players into 8 equal teams. Explain why this is not possible. Then tell a way he could divide the players into equal teams.

_____

_____

Answer _____ teams of _____ players each

Quiz 9: Solving Word Problems

1   Jen had 42 dimes and Meg had 18 dimes. They used all their dimes to buy hair clips for 5 dimes each. How many hair clips did Jen and Meg buy?

Ⓐ 12   Ⓑ 14   Ⓒ 65   Ⓓ 70

2   Devlin earns $7 for each hour he works. He worked for 6 hours, and was also given tips of $35. How much did Devlin earn in all?

Ⓐ $42   Ⓑ $48   Ⓒ $71   Ⓓ $77

3   A store had 42 muffins at the start of the day and 8 muffins left unsold at the end of the day. Each muffin sold for $2. How much money was made from the sale of the muffins that day?

Ⓐ $36   Ⓑ $58   Ⓒ $68   Ⓓ $100

4   Sam bought 6 packets of 10 pens. He divided the pens into 4 equal groups. How many pens were in each group?

Ⓐ 4   Ⓑ 12   Ⓒ 15   Ⓓ 20

5   The table shows how many cans students collected for a recycling drive.

	Denzel	Hudson	Colin	Garth	Sanjay	Wes
Number of Cans	44	14	18	62	26	32

Which two students collected the same total amount of cans as Garth? _____ and _____

Which two students collected the same total amount of cans as Hudson and Garth combined? _____ and _____

The goal of the recycling drive was to collect 200 cans. How many more cans need to be collected to reach the goal? _____

6   A chef buys 4 boxes of apples. Each box has 3 layers of apples, and there are 20 apples in each layer. How many apples did the chef buy?

Show your work.

Answer _____ apples

7   Bradford had $35 in savings. He then saved $8 each week for 6 weeks. How much money did Bradford have at the end of 6 weeks?

Show your work.

Answer $_____

8   A chef has 12 apple pies. Each apple pie has 8 serves. The chef serves 54 pieces of apple pie. How many pieces of apple pie are left over?

Show your work.

Answer _____ pieces of pie

9   Jeremy is making 6 photo frames. He needs 10 nails for each photo frame. He buys the nails in packs of 15. How many packs of nails does he need?

Show your work.

Answer _____ packs of nails

10   Maurice has $40 in savings. He plans to save $6 each week. How many weeks will it take for Maurice to have a total of over $80? Use pictures, words, or math to explain the work needed to find the answer.

Answer _____ weeks

11   Jo read that a kitten's weight increases by about 30 grams each day for the first 10 days. When Jo's cat had a kitten, it weighed 110 grams. How much would Jo expect the kitten to weigh after 10 days of growth? Use pictures, words, or math to explain the work needed to find the answer.

Answer _____ grams

12   Andrew buys 6 cartons of water, with 8 bottles of water in each carton. If he drinks 3 bottles of water each day, how long will all the water last? Use pictures, words, or math to explain the work needed to find the answer.

Answer _____ days

13   The sign below shows the price of fruits at a store.

Bananas	Oranges	Apples	Pears
4 for $3	10 for $4	4 for $2	6 for $3

Ben spends $12 on oranges. How many oranges did he buy?

Show your work.

Answer _____ oranges

Kim buys 8 bananas, 12 apples, and 30 pears. What is the total cost?

Show your work.

Answer $_____

Sadie buys pears. She gives the cashier $20 and receives $8 change. How many pears did she buy?

Show your work.

Answer _____ pears

Harriet buys oranges and pears. She spends $14 and receives 32 pieces of fruit. How many oranges and pears did she buy?

Show your work.

Answer _____ oranges and _____ pears

Quiz 10: Representing Word Problems with Equations

1 Emilio organized 32 marbles into 4 equal piles. Which number sentence could be used to find the number of marbles in each pile?

Ⓐ 4 ÷ ___ = 32   Ⓑ 4 × ___ = 32

Ⓒ ___ + 4 = 32   Ⓓ ___ − 4 = 32

2 Max had 15 baseball cards. He bought 6 baseball cards. Then he lost 2 baseball cards. Which expression can be used to find the number of baseball cards Max has now?

Ⓐ 15 + 6 + 2   Ⓑ 15 + 6 − 2

Ⓒ 15 − 6 + 2   Ⓓ 15 − 6 − 2

3 During a sale, each television is on sale for $150 less than the normal price. Adam buys a television during the sale for $845. Which equation can be used to find the normal price of the television, p?

Ⓐ $p + 150 = 845$ Ⓑ $p - 150 = 845$

Ⓒ $845 - p = 150$ Ⓓ $150 + p = 845$

4 Julie had $10. She bought a drink for $2. She spent the rest of the money buying sandwiches for $4 each. Which equation can be used to find how many sandwiches she bought, s?

Ⓐ $10 + 2 = s \div 4$ Ⓑ $10 + 2 = 4 \times s$

Ⓒ $10 - 2 = s \div 4$ Ⓓ $10 - 2 = 4 \times s$

5 Ursula sells T-shirts for $8 each. She made $72 selling T-shirts. Which number sentences could be used to find how many T-shirts she sold, n? Select all the correct answers.

☐ $72 \div n = 8$ ☐ $72 \div 8 = n$

☐ $8 \times n = 72$ ☐ $n \times 8 = 72$

☐ $8 \div n = 72$ ☐ $8 \times 72 = n$

6   A store sells milkshakes for $4 each. Match the problem with the expression that can be used to solve it. Draw lines to show the matches.

Bill buys 5 milkshakes. What is the total cost? $20 ÷ 4 = 5$

How much change should you get if you pay for
1 milkshake with a $5 bill? $5 + 4 = 9$

Erin has $20. How many milkshakes can Erin buy? $5 × 4 = 20$

Lloyd buys 1 milkshake and a cookie for $5. What
is the total amount Lloyd spent? $5 - 4 = 1$

7   Write an equation to match each statement. Then find the missing number. The first one has been completed for you.

Statement	Equation	Missing Number
6 more than a number is equal to 14	___ + 6 = 14	8
a number times 5 is equal to 45		
12 less than a number is equal to 20		
20 divided by a number is equal to 4		
the sum of a number and 13 is equal to 30		
a number divided by 10 is equal to 5		
a number less 4 is equal to 24		
the product of a number and 7 is 28		

8   Jarred organized chairs into 6 rows of 9 chairs each and had 2 chairs left over. Write the correct symbols in the expression to show how to find the total number of chairs, *c*.

$$6 \:\boxed{}\: 9 \:\boxed{}\: 2 = c$$

9   Nerida has 62 pennies. She finds another 48 pennies. She uses the pennies to buy a pencil case for 85 pennies. Complete the equation to show how many pennies she has left, *p*. Then solve the equation to find the answer.

_____ + _____ - _____ = *p*

Answer _____ pennies

10   Samuel plans to study for 120 minutes. He wants to study math for 60 minutes, history for 20 minutes, and science for the rest of the time. Complete the equation to show how many minutes, *m*, he can study science for. Then solve the equation to find the answer.

_____ + _____ + *m* = _____

Answer _____ minutes

11   Kylar has to learn a total of 80 French words for a test. He has already learned 30 words. He wants to learn 5 new words every day. Complete the equation to show how many more days, *d*, he needs to study to learn the 80 words. Then solve the equation to find the answer.

(_____ - _____) ÷ _____ = *d*

Answer _____ days

12   Stefan is driving 380 miles to visit his uncle. He drove 170 miles before stopping for breakfast, and then another 140 miles before stopping for lunch. Write an equation to show how to find the number of miles he has left to drive, *m*. Then solve the equation to find the answer.

Answer _____ miles

13   Connor needs 36 white tiles and 28 black tiles to cover his back porch. The tiles are sold in boxes of 4. Write an equation to show how to find the number of boxes of tiles he needs to buy, *b*. Then solve the equation to find the answer.

Answer _____ boxes of tiles

14   Zeke plays basketball. Write an equation to represent each problem. Use *x* as the missing value. Then solve the equation to find the answer.

Zeke's team scored 86 points. Zeke scored 22 of those points. How many points did the other players score?

Equation   **Answer** _____ points

Zeke has 3 practices of equal length and practices for a total of 120 minutes. How long is each practice session?

Equation   **Answer** _____ minutes

Zeke had 12 free throw attempts and made 9 of them. How many free throws did he miss?

Equation   **Answer** _____ free throws

Zeke's team scored 86 points, and won the game by 9 points. What was the other team's score?

Equation   **Answer** _____ points

Quiz 11: Using Estimation and Rounding

1   Which is the best way to estimate the sum of 87 and 58?

   Ⓐ 80 + 50   Ⓑ 90 + 50   Ⓒ 80 + 60   Ⓓ 90 + 60

2   Which is the best way to estimate the difference of 562 and 84?

   Ⓐ 560 – 80   Ⓑ 560 – 90   Ⓒ 570 – 80   Ⓓ 570 – 90

3   The table shows how many cans each class collected for a food drive.

Class	Number of Cans
Miss Peterson	87
Mr. Yuri	54
Mrs. Duncan	75

   Which is the best estimate of the total number of cans collected?

   Ⓐ 80 + 50 + 70 = 200   Ⓑ 80 + 50 + 80 = 210

   Ⓒ 90 + 50 + 80 = 220   Ⓓ 90 + 60 + 80 = 230

4   A school has 237 third grade students, 369 fourth grade students, and 325 fifth grade students. Which number sentence shows the best way to estimate the total number of students?

   Ⓐ 200 + 300 + 300 = 800   Ⓑ 200 + 400 + 400 = 1,000

   Ⓒ 200 + 400 + 300 = 900   Ⓓ 300 + 400 + 400 = 1,100

5   Tara sells 42 cupcakes for $3 each. Which is the best estimate of the total amount she made?

   Ⓐ $40   Ⓑ $120   Ⓒ $150   Ⓓ $200

6   Trey has 58 game tokens to divide evenly between 8 friends. What is the greatest number of game tokens he could give to each friend?

   Ⓐ 6   Ⓑ 7   Ⓒ 8   Ⓓ 9

7 Round the two-digit number up and down to find two numbers the product will be between. Then complete the sentence. The first one has been completed for you.

63×7 $60 \times 7 = 420$ $70 \times 7 = 490$

The product of 63 and 7 will be between 420 and 490.

71×3 _____ $\times 3 =$ _____   _____ $\times 3 =$ _____

The product of 71 and 3 will be between _____ and _____.

26×5 _____ $\times 5 =$ _____   _____ $\times 5 =$ _____

The product of 26 and 5 will be between _____ and _____.

87×6 _____ $\times 6 =$ _____   _____ $\times 6 =$ _____

The product of 87 and 6 will be between _____ and _____.

8 The school library has 1,412 fiction books, 1,845 non-fiction books, and 1,183 children's books. Answer each question by rounding each number to the nearest hundred and then completing the calculation.

About how many more non-fiction books are there than children's books?

_____ - _____ = _____

Answer _____ books

About how many more non-fiction books are there than fiction books?

_____ - _____ = _____

Answer _____ books

About how many books are there in all?

_____ + _____ + _____ = _____

Answer _____ books

9   Mr. Oliver has $1000 to spend on office equipment. The list below shows what he plans to buy.

- 1 printer that costs $275.
- 1 scanner that costs $218.
- 1 laptop that costs $369.

Round the cost of each item to the nearest ten.

Printer $_____   Scanner $_____   Laptop $_____

Use the rounded amounts to find about how much money Mr. Oliver will have left if he buys the three items.

Show your work.

Answer $_____

10   A car traveled 189 miles in 3 hours. About how many miles did the car travel each hour?

Show your work.

Answer _____ miles

11   A theater has 497 seats. People are sitting in 352 of the seats. About how many seats are empty?

Show your work.

Answer _____ seats

12   The table below shows how many visitors a zoo had on three days.

Day	Number of People
Friday	237
Saturday	258
Sunday	198

About how many visitors did the zoo have over the three days? Round each number to the nearest ten to find the answer.

Show your work.

Answer _____ visitors

Each visitor bought a $20 ticket to visit the zoo. On which day did the zoo make closest to $4,000 in ticket sales? Show your work or explain how you found the answer.

Answer _____

13   Ricky saved $8 each week for 32 weeks. Would he have saved just under $240 or just over $240? Explain your answer.

_____

_____

14   Darius says that the product of 4 and 9 must be less than 40. Explain why Darius is correct.

_____

_____

Quiz 12: Understanding Patterns

1   Which number comes next in the pattern below?

2, 5, 8, 11, 14, ...

Ⓐ 16   Ⓑ 17   Ⓒ 20   Ⓓ 25

2   If *n* is a number in the pattern, which rule can be used to find the next number in the pattern?

4, 6, 8, 10, 12, 14, 16, ...

Ⓐ $n + 2$ Ⓑ $n - 2$ Ⓒ $n + 4$ Ⓓ $n - 4$

3   A florist makes bunches of flowers by placing 4 flowers together and tying them with 1 piece of ribbon. Which expression can be used to find the number of flowers used if 8 pieces of ribbon are used?

Ⓐ 8 ÷ 4   Ⓑ 8 + 4   Ⓒ 8 × 4   Ⓓ 8 - 4

4   The table below shows the relationship between the number of tables set in a restaurant and the number of napkins used.

Number of Tables	3	6	9	12	15
Number of Napkins	24	48		96	120

Based on the pattern, which number sentence can be used to find the number of napkins needed to set 9 tables?

Ⓐ 96 ÷ 2   Ⓑ 9 × 24   Ⓒ 42 × 2   Ⓓ 9 × 8

5   Brook is 14 years old. Chad has the same birth date, but is 7 years younger. When Brook is 18 years old, how old will Chad be?

Ⓐ 9 years old   Ⓑ 11 years old   Ⓒ 15 years old   Ⓓ 21 years old

6   Jasper has 14 baseball cards. He buys more baseball cards in packets of 4 baseball cards each. Complete the pattern that shows how many baseball cards Jasper could have.

14, _____, _____, _____, _____, _____, _____

7   The first six numbers in a pattern are shown below. Which statement is true about every number in the pattern?

5, 10, 15, 20, 25, 30, …

Ⓐ It is divisible by 5.   Ⓑ It is a multiple of 10.

Ⓒ It is an odd number.   Ⓓ It is an even number.

8   Fill in the blanks to describe each pattern below.

Pattern	Description
2, 5, 8, 11, 14, 17, …	The pattern starts at _____. Each number is _____ more than the one before it.
3, 6, 12, 24, 48, …	The pattern starts at _____. Each number is _____ times more than the one before it.
40, 36, 32, 28, 24, …	The pattern starts at _____. Each number is _____ less than the one before it.
1, 6, 11, 16, 21, 26, …	The pattern starts at _____. Each number is _____ more than the one before it.
100, 89, 78, 67, 56, …	The pattern starts at _____. Each number is _____ less than the one before it.
1, 4, 16, 64, 256, …	The pattern starts at _____. Each number is _____ times more than the one before it.

9   For each pattern, write an expression that can be used to find the next number in the pattern. Use *n* to represent the last number in the pattern. Then complete the missing numbers.

Pattern	Expression
Pattern	**Expression**
6, 9, 12, 15, 18, 21, _____, _____	*n* + 3
6, 10, 14, 18, 22, _____, _____	
48, 42, 36, 30, 24, _____, _____	
64, 32, 16, 8, _____, _____	
1, 2, 4, 8, 16, _____, _____	

10   Sort the patterns described below into those that will have only odd numbers, those that will have only even numbers, and those that will have both. List the letters in the table to show your answers.

A   starts at 5, adds 4 to each number
B   starts at 80, subtracts 3 from each number
C   starts at 2, each number is twice the one before it
D   starts at 5, adds 7 to each number
E   starts at 35, each number is 6 less than the one before it
F   starts at 16, adds 9 to each number
G   starts at 1, each number is 3 times the one before it
H   starts at 10, each number is 8 more than the one before it
I   starts at 3, each number is twice the one before it
J   starts at 4, multiplies each number by 10

Patterns with Only Odd Numbers	Patterns with Only Even Numbers	Patterns with Odd and Even Numbers

11   A bakery sells its rolls in bags of 8 for $3 each bag. Complete the table.

Number of Bags of Rolls	Total Number of Rolls	Total Cost ($)
2		
3		
4		
5		
6		

Explain why the total number of rolls will always be even.

_____

_____

Explain why the total cost is not always even.

_____

_____

12   Apple trees were planted in rows. Each row had the same number of apple trees. Complete the missing numbers in the table below.

Number of Rows	4	5	6	7	8	9	10
Number of Trees	24	30	36				

Explain why the total number of apple trees will always be a multiple of 6.

_____

_____

Quizzes 13 to 18

Number and Operations in Base Ten

Directions

Read each question carefully. For each multiple-choice question, fill in the circle for the correct answer. For other types of questions, follow the directions given in the question.

You may use a ruler to help you answer questions. You should answer the questions without using a calculator.

COMMON CORE SKILLS LIST
For Parents, Teachers, and Tutors

Quizzes 13 through 18 cover these skills from the Common Core State Standards.

Number and Operations in Base Ten

Use place value understanding and properties of operations to perform multi-digit arithmetic.

1. Use place value understanding to round whole numbers to the nearest 10 or 100.

2. Fluently add and subtract within 1000 using strategies and algorithms based on place value, properties of operations, and/or the relationship between addition and subtraction.

3. Multiply one-digit whole numbers by multiples of 10 in the range 10–90 (e.g., 9 × 80, 5 × 60) using strategies based on place value and properties of operations.

Quiz 13: Understanding and Using Place Value

1   There are 709 students at Mike's school. Which of these is another way to write 709?

Ⓐ 7 + 9   Ⓑ 70 + 9   Ⓒ 700 + 9   Ⓓ 700 + 90

2   Which number has a 7 in the hundreds place?

Ⓐ 7,386   Ⓑ 3,879   Ⓒ 2,782   Ⓓ 1,937

3   Which number is represented by the diagram below?

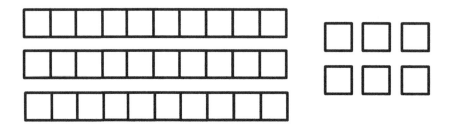

Ⓐ 18   Ⓑ 36   Ⓒ 180   Ⓓ 360

4   Which digit in the number 4,829 proves that the number is greater than 4,357?

Ⓐ 4   Ⓑ 8   Ⓒ 2   Ⓓ 9

5   Circle all the numbers that have a 6 in the tens place.

| 36 | 67 | 16 | 60 |

| 680 | 206 | 365 | 600 |

| 1,674 | 6,087 | 5,364 | 3,426 |

6   Which expression could be used to find the sum of 256 and 71?

    Ⓐ 2 + 5 + 6 + 7 + 1   Ⓑ 20 + 50 + 6 + 70 + 1

    Ⓒ 200 + 700 + 50 + 6 + 1   Ⓓ 200 + 50 + 70 + 6 + 1

7   Write numbers on the lines to complete each sentence correctly.

    89 is the same as _____ tens and _____ ones.

    65 is the same as _____ tens and _____ ones.

    42 is the same as _____ tens and _____ ones.

    975 is the same as _____ hundreds, _____ tens, and _____ ones.

    703 is the same as _____ hundreds, _____ tens, and _____ ones.

    540 is the same as _____ hundreds, _____ tens, and _____ ones.

8   Fill in the chart to show how many hundreds, tens, and ones are in each number.

Number	Hundreds	Tens	Ones
684			
759			
403			
160			

9   Write numbers on the lines to show each number in expanded form.

    682   (___ × 100) + (___ × 10) + (___ × 1)

    295   (___ × 100) + (___ × 10) + (___ × 1)

    304   (___ × 100) + (___ × 10) + (___ × 1)

    570   (___ × 100) + (___ × 10) + (___ × 1)

10   Choose one number from each column to create each three-digit number described. Write the number on the blank line.

Hundreds	Tens	Ones
6	9	3
9	5	5
7	4	8
1	3	9

An even number greater than 980. _____

The lowest three-digit number possible. _____

The greatest three-digit number possible. _____

A number between 740 and 744. _____

A number less than 140 that is divisible by 5. _____

A number greater than 654 but less than 657. _____

A number 10 greater than 148. _____

A number 100 less than 759. _____

11   Write the correct number on each blank line.

Which number is ten less than 458? _____

Which number is two hundreds more than 365? _____

Which number is six more than 421? _____

Which number is three tens more than 147? _____

Which number is five hundreds less than 786? _____

Which number is one less than 564? _____

Which number is one hundred less than 836? _____

Which number is seven tens less than 978? _____

12 Complete the missing number to make each number sentence correct.

262 + _____ = 282   385 + _____ = 985   85 – _____ = 73

197 + _____ = 597   799 – _____ = 709   43 + _____ = 68

350 – _____ = 310   408 + _____ = 478   11 + _____ = 45

485 – _____ = 185   512 – _____ = 112   64 – _____ = 13

897 + _____ = 899   957 + _____ = 987   57 – _____ = 22

13 What are the two smallest 3-digit numbers that can be made using the digits 6, 3, and 7? Each digit must be used only once in each number.

Answer _____ and _____

On the lines below, explain how you found your answer.

_____

_____

_____

14 Sal estimates the sum of 1,274 and 3,426 by rounding each number to the nearest ten. Alex estimates the sum of 1,274 and 3,426 by rounding each number to the nearest hundred. Whose estimate is closest to the exact sum of the numbers? Explain your answer.

_____

_____

_____

Quiz 14: Rounding Whole Numbers

1   What is 687 rounded to the nearest ten?

Ⓐ 600   Ⓑ 680   Ⓒ 690   Ⓓ 700

2   What is 374 rounded to the nearest hundred?

Ⓐ 300   Ⓑ 370   Ⓒ 380   Ⓓ 400

3   Select all the numbers that will equal 650 when rounded to the nearest ten.

☐ 643   ☐ 637   ☐ 647

☐ 659   ☐ 653   ☐ 665

☐ 652   ☐ 605   ☐ 651

4   Select all the numbers that will equal 800 when rounded to the nearest hundred.

☐ 842   ☐ 803   ☐ 861

☐ 870   ☐ 848   ☐ 817

☐ 894   ☐ 826   ☐ 855

5   What is 774 rounded to the nearest ten and nearest hundred?

Nearest ten _____   Nearest hundred _____

6   What is 1,227 rounded to the nearest ten and nearest hundred?

Nearest ten _____   Nearest hundred _____

7 Complete the table by rounding each number to the nearest 10 and the nearest 100.

Number	Nearest 10	Nearest 100
687		
524		
186		
359		
62		
725		
133		
805		
261		
909		

8 Complete the table by writing in a possible number for the original number.

Number	Nearest 10	Nearest 100
	430	400
	90	100
	680	700
	130	100
	110	100
	190	200
	690	700
	460	500
	340	300
	710	700

9   Complete each statement that describes which digit is used to decide whether to round the number up or down.

681 to the nearest ten   the digit ____, which is in the _____ place

7,486 to the nearest ten   the digit ____, which is in the _____ place

547 to the nearest hundred   the digit ____, which is in the _____ place

1,352 to the nearest hundred   the digit ____, which is in the _____ place

10   On the number line below, plot all the whole numbers that equal 90 when rounded to the nearest ten.

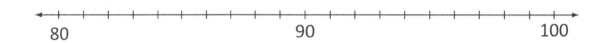

80   90   100

11   Complete the table by filling in the missing numbers.

Number Rounded to the Nearest Ten	Lowest Possible Number	Highest Possible Number
50		
280		
400		
1,760		

12   Round 8,782 to the nearest ten and the nearest hundred.

Nearest ten _____   Nearest hundred _____

Explain how you worked out whether to round the number up or down.

_____

_____

13 The table shows how many points Greg's basketball team scored in each game. Greg rounds the scores to the nearest ten.

Game	1	2	3	4	5	6	7	8
Score	87	76	92	72	81	66	94	79

In which two games did the team score 70 points, to the nearest ten?

_____ and _____

In which three games did the team score 90 points, to the nearest ten?

_____, _____, and _____

In the next game, the score to the nearest ten was 60. What is the most the actual score could be? Explain your answer.

_____

_____

To estimate the total points scored, Greg rounds all the scores to the nearest hundred and adds them. Would the estimate be more or less than the actual total points scored? Explain your answer.

_____

_____

14 Michael states that to the nearest hundred, there are 700 students at his school. Jessica states that there must be at least 700 students, but no more than 749 students. Describe the mistake that Jessica made.

_____

_____

_____

Quiz 15: Adding Whole Numbers

1   Juan read 42 pages of a book on Monday. He read another 39 pages of the book on Tuesday. How many pages did he read in all?

Ⓐ 70   Ⓑ 71   Ⓒ 80   Ⓓ 81

2   Mr. Wilkins drove 162 miles on Monday. Then he drove 138 miles on Tuesday. How many miles did he drive in all?

Ⓐ 200 miles   Ⓑ 300 miles   Ⓒ 310 miles   Ⓓ 290 miles

3   Sienna's school has 348 third grade students, 312 fourth grade students, and 306 fifth grade students. How many students are there in all?

Ⓐ 954   Ⓑ 956   Ⓒ 964   Ⓓ 966

4   Complete the addition problems below.

| 626 + | 145 + | 357 + | 405 + |
| 153 | 234 | 349 | 205 |

| 750 + | 723 + | 447 + | 215 + |
| 164 | 107 | 462 | 385 |

| 425 + | 508 + | 626 + | 250 + |
| 153 | 262 | 183 | 350 |

| 206 + | 492 + | 525 + | 708 + |
| 204 | 208 | 315 | 152 |

5   Which expressions have a sum of 100? Select all the correct answers.

☐ 73 + 37   ☐ 3 + 82 + 15

☐ 18 + 84   ☐ 62 + 28 + 10

☐ 52 + 48   ☐ 75 + 25 + 25

6   Which sum has the greatest value? Select the one correct answer.

☐ 158 + 292   ☐ 130 + 295   ☐ 305 + 88

☐ 244 + 213   ☐ 212 + 218   ☐ 327 + 41

7   For each expression, complete the missing number to show two expressions with the same value.

(46 + 19) + 12   (12 + ____) + 46   (46 + ____) + 19

(33 + 89) + 66   (33 + ____) + 89   (66 + ____) + 33

(67 + 55) + 23   (____ + 67) + 55   (____ + 23) + 67

(71 + 27) + 44   (27 + 44) + ____   (44 + 71) + ____

8   For each addition equation, complete the two subtraction equations that could be used to check the answer.

35 + 44 = 79   ____ - ____ = ____   ____ - ____ = ____

77 + 52 = 129   ____ - ____ = ____   ____ - ____ = ____

24 + 89 = 113   ____ - ____ = ____   ____ - ____ = ____

152 + 141 = 293   ____ - ____ = ____   ____ - ____ = ____

305 + 285 = 590   ____ - ____ = ____   ____ - ____ = ____

641 + 111 = 752   ____ - ____ = ____   ____ - ____ = ____

9   For each addition problem below, complete the calculation in steps. In the first step, add the tens. In the second step, add the ones. In the third step, add the sum of the tens and the ones. The first one has been completed.

Problem	Step 1: Add the Tens	Step 2: Add the Ones	Step 3: Add the Two Sums
42 + 85	40 + 80 = 120	2 + 5 = 7	120 + 7 = 127
63 + 19	____ + ____ = ____	____ + ____ = ____	____ + ____ = ____
27 + 48	____ + ____ = ____	____ + ____ = ____	____ + ____ = ____
31 + 26	____ + ____ = ____	____ + ____ = ____	____ + ____ = ____
75 + 17	____ + ____ = ____	____ + ____ = ____	____ + ____ = ____
58 + 38	____ + ____ = ____	____ + ____ = ____	____ + ____ = ____

10   Dan is training for a bike race. He rode 18 miles on Monday, 19 miles on Tuesday, and 12 miles on Wednesday. How far did he ride in all?

Show your work.

Answer _____ miles

11   A zoo had 586 visitors on Saturday and 421 visitors on Sunday. How many visitors did the zoo have on the weekend?

Show your work.

Answer _____ visitors

12   Sam has 111 stamps in her collection. Courtney has 182 more stamps in her collection than Sam. How many stamps does Courtney have?

Show your work.

Answer _____ stamps

How many stamps do Sam and Courtney have together?

Show your work.

Answer _____ stamps

13   Janet wants to find the sum of the three numbers below. Janet first adds the numbers 138 and 262. Then she adds 85 to the result. Complete the equations to show the two steps.

Sum of 138, 85, 262   138 + 262 = _____   _____ + 85 = _____

Explain why the calculation is easier if 138 and 262 are added first.

_____

_____

14   For each set of numbers below, choose the two numbers to add first. Then add the third number to the result to show the total sum.

Sum of 65, 47, 35   ____ + ____ = ____   ____ + ____ = ____

Sum of 29, 71, 34   ____ + ____ = ____   ____ + ____ = ____

Sum of 88, 67, 32   ____ + ____ = ____   ____ + ____ = ____

Sum of 57, 26, 44   ____ + ____ = ____   ____ + ____ = ____

Quiz 16: Subtracting Whole Numbers

1   Heath scored 87 on a reading test. Rima scored 18 points less than Heath. How many points did Rima score?

    Ⓐ 61   Ⓑ 69   Ⓒ 71   Ⓓ 79

2   Jackson had $96 in savings. He spent $18 on a present for his brother. How much money does Jackson have left?

    Ⓐ $74   Ⓑ $78   Ⓒ $84   Ⓓ $88

3   Mr. Piper has to drive a total of 582 miles. He drove 291 miles on the first day. How far does Mr. Piper have left to drive?

    Ⓐ 211 miles   Ⓑ 291 miles   Ⓒ 311 miles   Ⓓ 391 miles

4   Complete the subtractions problems below.

589 - 47	380 - 55	218 - 39	743 - 88
852 - 321	468 - 109	905 - 175	557 - 519
608 - 205	755 - 355	608 - 253	584 - 106
835 - 204	465 - 305	912 - 509	667 - 390

5   Which expressions have a difference of 4? Select all the correct answers.

☐ 108 − 102   ☐ 355 − 301   ☐ 100 − 64 − 32

☐ 289 − 285   ☐ 88 − 42 − 42   ☐ 845 − 800 − 45

6   Which difference is equal to 30? Select the one correct answer.

☐ 689 - 389   ☐ 689 - 359   ☐ 689 - 356

☐ 689 - 659   ☐ 689 - 686   ☐ 689 - 656

7   Which number is 40 less than 589? _____

Which number is 200 less than 589? _____

Which number is 240 less than 589? _____

8   For each expression, complete the missing numbers to show an expression with the same value.

(88 - 15) - 22   (88 - _____) - _____

(175 - 39) - 67   (175 - _____) - _____

(412 - 58) - 73   (412 - _____) - _____

9   For each subtraction equation, complete an addition equation that could be used to check the answer.

159 − 86 = 73   _____ + _____ = _____

365 − 99 = 266   _____ + _____ = _____

274 − 178 = 96   _____ + _____ = _____

867 − 745 = 122   _____ + _____ = _____

907 − 138 = 769   _____ + _____ = _____

750 − 425 = 325   _____ + _____ = _____

10 Alvin is 136 centimeters tall. Sara is 16 centimeters shorter than Alvin. How tall is Sara?

Show your work.

Answer _____ centimeters

11 The normal price of a computer is $790. During a sale, the computer is $150 less than the normal price. What is the sale price of the computer?

Show your work.

Answer $_____

12 At Emiko's school, there are 247 students in third grade. There are 29 fewer students in fourth grade. How many students are in fourth grade?

Show your work.

Answer _____ students

13 Carol had $500 to spend on office furniture. She bought a new desk for $259 and a new bookcase for $188. How much does Carol have left?

Show your work.

Answer $_____

14   Juan had $128 in his savings account. He spent $6 every week for 4 weeks. How much money would be in his savings account after 4 weeks?

Show your work.

Answer $_____

15   A school cafeteria offered four Italian meal choices. The table below shows the number of meals served of each type.

Meal	Number Served
Pasta	151
Pizza	167
Salad	213
Risotto	117

How many more salad meals were served than risotto meals?

Show your work.

Answer _____ meals

The school hoped to sell a total of 1,000 meals. How many more meals needed to be sold to reach this goal?

Show your work.

Answer _____ meals

Quiz 17: Adding and Subtracting Whole Numbers

1   Porter has 945 sheep in three fields. There are 185 sheep in the first field and 428 sheep in the second field. How many sheep are in the third field?

Ⓐ 332   Ⓑ 517   Ⓒ 613   Ⓓ 702

2   Leon had $138 in savings. He spent $27 at the bookstore. Then he was given $15 by his grandmother. How much money does Leon have now?

Ⓐ $106   Ⓑ $126   Ⓒ $150   Ⓓ $180

3   Audrey states that if she sells 68 pretzels, there will be 14 pretzels left. Which number sentence can be used to find the total number of pretzels she has?

Ⓐ 68 + ___ = 14   Ⓑ 14 + ___ = 68   Ⓒ 68 - ___ = 14   Ⓓ ___ - 68 = 14

4   Which expressions can be used to find the sum of 106 and 35? Select all the correct answers.

☐ (100 + 300) + (6 + 5)   ☐ 100 + (60 + 30) + 5   ☐ 100 + 30 + (6 + 5)

☐ (10 + 30) + (6 + 5)   ☐ (100 + 35) + 6   ☐ (100 + 5) + 30

5   Place the expressions below in order from smallest to greatest.
Write the numbers 1, 2, 3, and 4 on the lines to show the order.

___ 584 + 36   ___ 584 + 63   ___ 584 - 36   ___ 584 - 63

6   A school printed 1,000 comics. Teachers were given 20 comics, students were given 840 comics, and 40 comics were given to the library. Complete the expressions to show two ways to find how many comics were left.

Expression _____ - _____ - _____ - _____ = _____

Expression _____ - (_____ + _____ + _____) = _____

7   The table shows the sales a drink stand made one day.

Size	Apple Juice	Lemonade
Small	36	39
Medium	49	68
Large	57	71

How many drinks were sold in all?

Show your work.

Answer _____ drinks

How many more lemonades were sold than apple juices?

Show your work.

Answer _____ drinks

8   Belinda needs to finish reading a book with 150 pages.

- She read 26 pages on Monday.
- She read 42 pages on Tuesday.
- She read 34 pages on Wednesday.

How many more pages does she need to read to finish the book?

Show your work.

Answer _____ pages

9   The table shows how many books a store sold each day of the week.

Day	Number of Book Sales
Monday	166
Tuesday	121
Wednesday	134
Thursday	139
Friday	145
Saturday	268
Sunday	212

On which two days did the store have a total of 260 sales?

_____ and _____

On which two days did the store have a total of 300 sales?

_____ and _____

How many sales did the store have on Saturday and Sunday?

_____ sales

How many more sales did the store have on Friday than on Thursday?

_____ sales

What is the difference in sales between the day with the most sales and the day with the least sales?

_____ sales

Complete the addition equation to show that the store had twice as many sales on Saturday as on Wednesday.

_____ + _____ = _____

10   Lana buys a box of 100 beads. She uses the beads to make jewelry.

- • She uses 18 beads to make each bracelet.
- • She uses 24 beads to make each necklace.
- • She uses 8 beads to make each anklet.

She makes 2 bracelets, 1 necklace, and 1 anklet. How many beads does she use?

Show your work.

Answer _____ beads

How many beads from the box of 100 are left over?

Show your work.

Answer _____ beads

Describe two different sets of items she could make to use all the remaining beads.

Show your work.

Answer _____ or _____

She buys another box of 100 beads. She makes 4 items and has exactly 4 beads left over. Which items did she make?

Show your work.

Answer _____

Quiz 18: Multiplying by Multiples of 10

1   What is the product of 6 and 80?

      Ⓐ 420   Ⓑ 480   Ⓒ 640   Ⓓ 680

2   What is the product of 5 and 50?

      Ⓐ 55   Ⓑ 225   Ⓒ 250   Ⓓ 550

3   Mitch has football training 3 times a week. Each training session goes for 40 minutes. How long does Mitch train for each week?

      Ⓐ 70 minutes   Ⓑ 80 minutes   Ⓒ 120 minutes   Ⓓ 140 minutes

4   Which expressions have a product of 360? Select all the correct answers.

      ☐ 4 × 90   ☐ 5 × 80   ☐ 7 × 50

      ☐ 6 × 60   ☐ 8 × 70   ☐ 9 × 40

5   Shayne practices piano for 30 minutes every day. Complete the table to show how long she practices in all after each number of days.

Number of Days	Total Number of Minutes
1	
2	
3	
4	
5	
6	
7	

6   Joanna is making picture frames. She uses 40 inches of timber to make each frame. How much timber would she use to make 9 picture frames?

Show your work.

Answer _____ inches

If she sells all 9 picture frames for $60 each, how much will she make?

Show your work.

Answer $_____

7   The table shows the number of stickers Gabby uses to make different numbers of gift cards.

Number of Gift Cards	3	4	5
Number of Stickers	60	80	100

How many stickers does Gabby use to make each gift card?

Show your work.

Answer _____ stickers

How many stickers would Gabby need to make 8 gift cards?

Show your work.

Answer _____ stickers

8   Tahlia has 10 vases to fill with flowers. She places 6 red roses and 2 yellow roses in each vase. How many roses did she use in all to fill the 10 vases?

Show your work.

Answer _____ roses

Tahlia adds white roses so that each vase has a total of 12 roses. How many white roses did she use?

Show your work.

Answer _____ white roses

9   There were 180 students in a fitness class. They were divided into 20 equal groups. Complete the number sentence that can be used to find how many students were in each group. Then use the number sentence to find the answer.

20 × _____ = 180

Answer _____ students

10   Mr. Ash has 240 markers. He divides them evenly between 30 students. Write a multiplication equation that can be used to find how many markers each student gets. Then solve the equation to find the answer.

Show your work.

Answer _____ markers

11   In a science contest, students received 10 points for each correct answer in the first round, 20 points for each correct answer in the second round, and 50 points for each correct answer in the final round. The table below shows the results for each student.

Student	Round 1 Correct Answers	Round 2 Correct Answers	Round 3 Correct Answers
Jayda	6	7	3
Brynn	10	5	2
Alana	4	8	1
Elly	9	4	3

Which student scored the same in Round 1 as in Round 2?

Show your work.

Answer _____

How many points were scored in Round 2 in all?

Show your work.

Answer _____ points

Place the students in order from the lowest total score to the highest total score. Write the student names on the lines to show your answer.

Show your work.

Lowest _____ _____ _____ _____ **Highest**

Quizzes 19 to 26

Number and Operations – Fractions

Directions

Read each question carefully. For each multiple-choice question, fill in the circle for the correct answer. For other types of questions, follow the directions given in the question.

You may use a ruler to help you answer questions. You should answer the questions without using a calculator.

COMMON CORE SKILLS LIST
For Parents, Teachers, and Tutors

Quizzes 19 through 26 cover these skills from the Common Core State Standards.

Number and Operations – Fractions

Develop understanding of fractions as numbers.

1. Understand a fraction 1/*b* as the quantity formed by 1 part when a whole is partitioned into *b* equal parts; understand a fraction *a*/*b* as the quantity formed by *a* parts of size 1/*b*.

2. Understand a fraction as a number on the number line; represent fractions on a number line diagram.
    a. Represent a fraction 1/*b* on a number line diagram by defining the interval from 0 to 1 as the whole and partitioning it into *b* equal parts. Recognize that each part has size 1/*b* and that the endpoint of the part based at 0 locates the number 1/*b* on the number line.
    b. Represent a fraction *a*/*b* on a number line diagram by marking off *a* lengths 1/*b* from 0. Recognize that the resulting interval has size *a*/*b* and that its endpoint locates the number *a*/*b* on the number line.

3. Explain equivalence of fractions in special cases, and compare fractions by reasoning about their size.
    a. Understand two fractions as equivalent (equal) if they are the same size, or the same point on a number line.
    b. Recognize and generate simple equivalent fractions, e.g., 1/2 = 2/4, 4/6 = 2/3. Explain why the fractions are equivalent, e.g., by using a visual fraction model.
    c. Express whole numbers as fractions, and recognize fractions that are equivalent to whole numbers.
    d. Compare two fractions with the same numerator or the same denominator by reasoning about their size. Recognize that comparisons are valid only when the two fractions refer to the same whole. Record the results of comparisons with the symbols >, =, or <, and justify the conclusions, e.g., by using a visual fraction model.

Quiz 19: Dividing into Equal Parts

1   What fraction of the figure below is shaded?

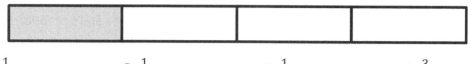

  Ⓐ $\frac{1}{2}$ Ⓑ $\frac{1}{3}$ Ⓒ $\frac{1}{4}$ Ⓓ $\frac{3}{4}$

2   Moira cut a length of ribbon into 3 equal pieces. What fraction of the whole is each piece?

  Ⓐ $\frac{1}{3}$ Ⓑ $\frac{3}{3}$ Ⓒ $\frac{1}{1}$ Ⓓ $\frac{3}{1}$

3   Justine divided a brownie into equal pieces, as shown below.

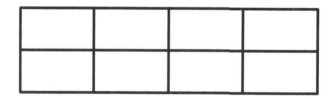

What fraction of the whole is each piece? _____

Justine ate 3 pieces. What fraction of the whole did Justine eat? _____

4   Draw lines to divide the rectangle below into 3 equal parts.

What fraction of the whole is each part? _____

5   Draw lines to divide the hexagon into 6 equal parts.

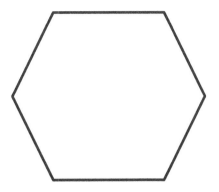

What fraction of the whole is each part? _____

6   Draw a line to divide each shape shown below into two equal halves.

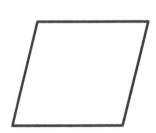  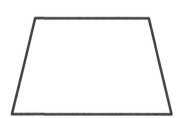

7   The shaded squares on the grid are a third of a shape. Shade squares to complete the whole shape.

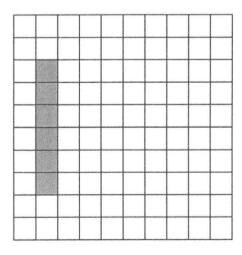

8   Sam has 16 candies. He divides them into 4 equal groups.

What fraction of the total candies is each group? _____

Joseph has 20 candies. He divides them into 4 equal groups.

What fraction of the total candies is each group? _____

Is there the same number of candies in each of Sam's groups as in each of Joseph's groups? Explain why or why not.

_____

_____

_____

9   Lennox divides a rectangle into two parts and shades one part, as shown.

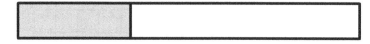

Lennox states that she has shaded $\frac{1}{2}$ the shape. Explain why Lennox's statement is incorrect.

_____

_____

_____

10   Divide the rectangle below into 8 equal areas. Shade $\frac{3}{8}$ of the rectangle.

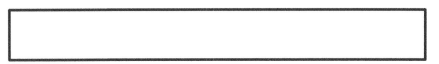

Divide the rectangle below into 4 equal areas. Shade $\frac{3}{4}$ of the rectangle.

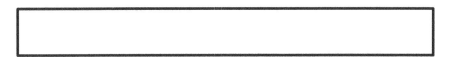

Use the shaded models to compare the fractions $\frac{3}{8}$ and $\frac{3}{4}$.

_____

_____

_____

11   The rectangle and hexagon below are both divided into 6 equal areas.

What fraction of the rectangle is shaded? _____

What fraction of the hexagon is shaded? _____

Is the shaded area of the rectangle equal to the shaded area of the hexagon? Explain why or why not.

_____

_____

_____

Quiz 20: Identifying Fractions

1   Which of these has $\frac{2}{3}$ shaded?

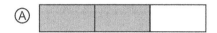   

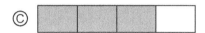   

2   Which diagram is shaded to represent $\frac{1}{4}$?

   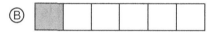

   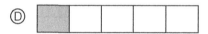

3   What fraction of the circle below is shaded?

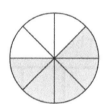

Ⓐ $\frac{5}{8}$ Ⓑ $\frac{3}{5}$ Ⓒ $\frac{2}{3}$ Ⓓ $\frac{3}{4}$

4   What fraction of the hexagon below is shaded?

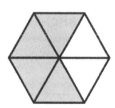

Ⓐ $\frac{2}{4}$ Ⓑ $\frac{3}{2}$ Ⓒ $\frac{2}{6}$ Ⓓ $\frac{2}{3}$

5   A pizza was cut into 8 equal pieces. The picture below shows the pieces of pizza left. What fraction of the pizza is left?

(A) $\frac{1}{8}$ (B) $\frac{1}{4}$ (C) $\frac{3}{4}$ (D) $\frac{3}{8}$

6   Which shapes have $\frac{1}{2}$ the squares shaded? Select all the correct answers.

☐ 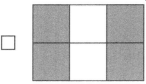   ☐

☐ 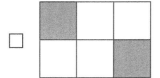   ☐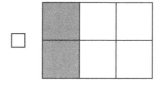

☐ 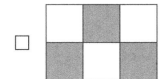   ☐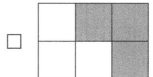

7   Vernon bought a carton of eggs and used 1 egg. The eggs left in the carton are shown below.

What fraction of the eggs are left in the carton? _____

8   Duncan's gas tank gauge shows how empty or full the tank is. Which statement describes the gas tank when the gauge is as below?

Ⓐ The gas tank is half full.

Ⓑ The gas tank is one quarter full.

Ⓒ The gas tank is three quarters full.

Ⓓ The gas tank is one third full.

9   For each shape below, shade the fraction of squares given.

$\dfrac{1}{2}$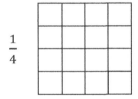

$\dfrac{1}{4}$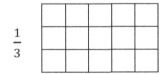

$\dfrac{1}{3}$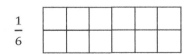

$\dfrac{1}{6}$

$\dfrac{1}{8}$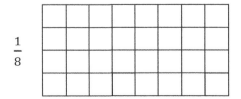

10   The flags of 12 different countries are shown below. Circle all the flags that are divided into equal thirds.

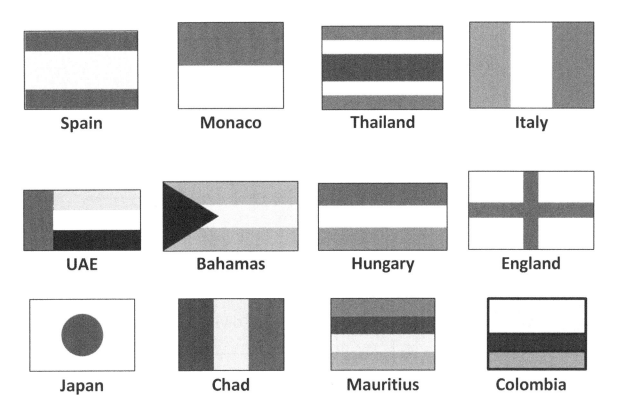

Which flag is divided into two equal halves? _____

Which flag is divided into four equal quarters? _____

11   Koby divided a triangle into equal pieces and then cut out one piece of the triangle, as shown below.

What fraction of the whole is the piece he cut out? _____

What fraction of the whole remains? _____

Quiz 21: Fractions and Number Lines

1   Which fraction is represented on the number line below?

Ⓐ $\frac{5}{6}$ Ⓑ $\frac{4}{5}$ Ⓒ $\frac{1}{6}$ Ⓓ $\frac{1}{5}$

2   Which fraction is represented on the number line below?

Ⓐ $\frac{2}{3}$ Ⓑ $\frac{2}{4}$ Ⓒ $\frac{2}{5}$ Ⓓ $\frac{2}{6}$

3   What fractions is the number line below divided into?

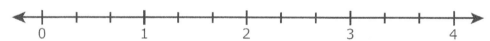

Ⓐ halves   Ⓑ thirds   Ⓒ quarters   Ⓓ eighths

4   Plot the fractions $\frac{1}{4}$, $\frac{1}{2}$, $1\frac{1}{4}$, and $1\frac{3}{4}$ on the number line below.

5   Divide the number line below into the same fractions as the rectangle below. Then plot the point that represents the fraction of the rectangle that is shaded.

6 Plot the fractions $\frac{1}{8}$, $\frac{4}{8}$, $\frac{5}{8}$, and $\frac{7}{8}$ on the number line below. Then use the number line to answer the questions below.

Which two fractions have a distance of $\frac{1}{8}$ between them? _____ and _____

Which two fractions have a distance of $\frac{2}{8}$ between them? _____ and _____

Which fraction is equivalent to $\frac{1}{2}$? _____

What is the distance between $\frac{7}{8}$ and 1? _____

7 Plot the fractions $\frac{1}{3}$, $1\frac{1}{3}$, $1\frac{2}{3}$, and $2\frac{1}{3}$ on the number line below. Then use the number line to answer the questions below.

Which two fractions have a distance of $\frac{1}{3}$ between them? _____ and _____

At which whole number would $\frac{3}{3}$ be plotted? _____

Which fraction plotted is closest to 1? _____

Which two fractions plotted would $\frac{2}{3}$ be plotted between? _____ and _____

What is the distance between $2\frac{1}{3}$ and 3? _____

8   Plot the fractions $\frac{1}{6}$, $\frac{2}{6}$, $\frac{5}{6}$, $1\frac{3}{6}$ and $1\frac{5}{6}$ on the number line below. Then use the number line to answer the questions below.

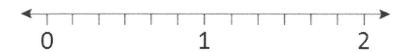

Which two fractions have a distance of $\frac{2}{6}$ between them? _____ and _____

Which fraction plotted is closest to 1? _____

Which fraction is equivalent to $\frac{1}{3}$? _____

Which fraction is equivalent to $1\frac{1}{2}$? _____

Which fraction plotted is $\frac{2}{3}$ less than 1? _____

What is the distance between $1\frac{5}{6}$ and 1? _____

9   The points on the number line represent the distances of four streets from Main Street. James Street is 1 mile from Main Street.

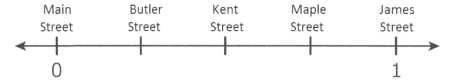

Which street is $\frac{1}{2}$ mile from Main Street? _____

Which street is $\frac{3}{4}$ mile from Main Street? _____

How far is the walk from Butler Street to Kent Street? _____ mile

How far is the walk from Kent Street to James Street? _____ mile

Which street is $\frac{1}{2}$ mile from Maple Street? _____

10   Plot the fractions listed on the number line below.

$$\frac{1}{2}, \frac{2}{3}, \frac{1}{6}, 1\frac{1}{3}, 1\frac{5}{6}$$

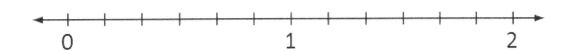

11   A charity run has checkpoints at equal distances. The number line below shows the distance of checkpoints A through G.

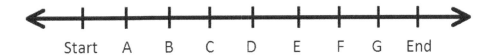

What fraction of the run is completed at Checkpoint A? _____

Explain how you found the answer on the lines below.

_____

_____

_____

At which checkpoint is half the run complete? _____

Explain how you found the answer on the lines below.

_____

_____

_____

Quiz 22: Understanding Equivalent Fractions

1   A number line is shown below.

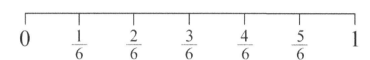

Which fraction on the number line is equivalent to $\frac{1}{3}$? _____

Which fraction on the number line is equivalent to $\frac{2}{3}$? _____

Which fraction on the number line is equivalent to $\frac{1}{2}$? _____

2   Shade the model below to show the fraction $\frac{4}{6}$.

Shade the model below to show a fraction equivalent to $\frac{4}{6}$.

What fraction is shaded above? _____

3   Circle all the fractions listed below that are equivalent.

$$\frac{2}{4} \qquad \frac{1}{3} \qquad \frac{3}{8} \qquad \frac{5}{6} \qquad \frac{4}{8} \qquad \frac{5}{8} \qquad \frac{2}{3} \qquad \frac{3}{6} \qquad \frac{1}{2}$$

4   Shade half of each model below. Then use the model to complete the fractions equivalent to $\frac{1}{2}$.

  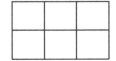 

$\frac{1}{2}$ $\frac{}{4}$ $\frac{}{6}$ $\frac{}{8}$

5   Shade the diagrams below to show the fraction $\frac{2}{3}$ and two fractions equivalent to $\frac{2}{3}$. Then write the equivalent fraction under each diagram.

$\frac{2}{3}$

6   Shade the diagrams below to show the fraction $\frac{1}{4}$ and a fraction equivalent to $\frac{1}{4}$. Then write the equivalent fraction under the second diagram.

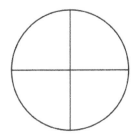 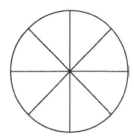

$\frac{1}{4}$

7   Aaron has quarters and dimes. Aaron's coins are shown below.

Complete the two fractions that show the fraction of coins that are quarters.

$$\frac{\boxed{}}{8} = \frac{\boxed{}}{4}$$

8   The number lines below have four points plotted.

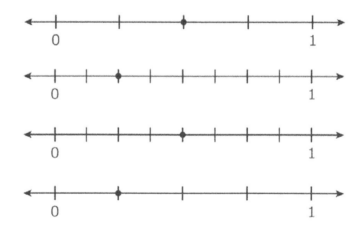

Write the two pairs of equivalent fractions on the lines below.

Answer _____ and _____, _____ and _____

Use the number lines to list a fraction that is equivalent to $\frac{3}{4}$.

Answer _____

9   Shade the diagrams below to show the fractions $\frac{1}{2}$, $\frac{2}{4}$, and $\frac{4}{8}$.

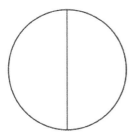 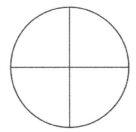 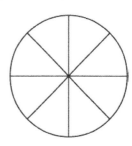

Explain how the diagrams show that the fractions are equivalent.

_____

_____

_____

_____

10   Divide the rectangles below into parts to show that $\frac{3}{4}$ is equivalent to $\frac{6}{8}$.

Explain how the diagrams show that the fractions are equivalent.

_____

_____

_____

_____

Quiz 23: Generating Equivalent Fractions

1   Which fraction is equivalent to $\frac{4}{6}$?

Ⓐ $\frac{2}{3}$ Ⓑ $\frac{1}{6}$ Ⓒ $\frac{1}{5}$ Ⓓ $\frac{1}{3}$

2   Which fraction is equivalent to the shaded area of the rectangle?

Ⓐ $\frac{4}{6}$ Ⓑ $\frac{2}{10}$ Ⓒ $\frac{2}{5}$ Ⓓ $\frac{1}{3}$

3   Doreen states that $\frac{6}{9}$ of the stars are shaded. Based on the diagram, what fraction of the stars are shaded?

Ⓐ $\frac{1}{6}$ Ⓑ $\frac{2}{3}$ Ⓒ $\frac{6}{3}$ Ⓓ $\frac{1}{2}$

4   Which fractions are equivalent to the shaded area of the circle? Select all the correct answers.

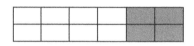

☐ $\frac{2}{6}$ ☐ $\frac{3}{6}$ ☐ $\frac{1}{3}$ ☐ $\frac{6}{6}$

☐ $\frac{1}{2}$ ☐ $\frac{3}{4}$ ☐ $\frac{1}{6}$ ☐ $\frac{2}{4}$

5 Which fraction can be placed in the empty box to make the statement below true?

$$\frac{6}{8} = \boxed{}$$

Ⓐ $\frac{2}{6}$ Ⓑ $\frac{3}{4}$ Ⓒ $\frac{2}{3}$ Ⓓ $\frac{3}{8}$

6 Which model is shaded to show a fraction equivalent to $\frac{2}{3}$?

Ⓐ

Ⓑ

Ⓒ

Ⓓ

7 Four fractions are shown below. Complete the fractions so that all four fractions are equivalent.

$$\frac{1}{} \qquad \frac{}{4} \qquad \frac{}{6} \qquad \frac{}{8}$$

8 A recipe uses $\frac{1}{4}$ teaspoon of vanilla. Complete the fractions below to show two fractions equivalent to $\frac{1}{4}$.

$$\frac{\boxed{}}{8} \quad \text{and} \quad \frac{4}{\boxed{}}$$

9   Jackson bought 4 chocolate cakes and 8 vanilla cakes.

Complete the fractions that show the fraction of cakes that are chocolate.

$$\frac{\boxed{}}{12} = \frac{\boxed{}}{6} = \frac{\boxed{}}{3}$$

10   Shade each figure below to show a fraction equivalent to $\frac{2}{8}$.

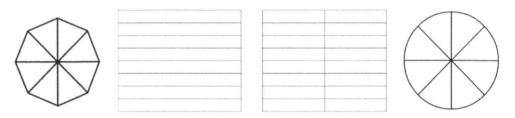

What fraction of each model is shaded? Write the fraction in lowest form.

Answer _____

11   Shade the fractions $\frac{1}{2}$ and $\frac{3}{6}$ on the fraction models below.

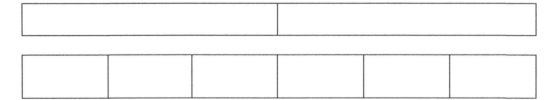

Shade the fraction model below to show another fraction equivalent to $\frac{1}{2}$ and $\frac{3}{6}$. Write the fraction on the line below.

What fraction did you shade? _____

12   Candice planted 15 plants in her garden. She planted 10 mint plants and 5 parsley plants, as represented below.

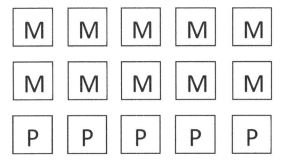

Complete the fractions to show the fraction of total plants that are mint and the fraction of total plants that are parsley in lowest terms.

Mint $\dfrac{10}{15} = \text{—}$ Parsley $\dfrac{5}{15} = \text{—}$

Candice wants to plant more parsley plants so that they make up $\frac{1}{2}$ the total plants. How many more parsley plants does she need? Show or explain how you found your answer.

Answer _____ plants

13   Quentin bought the bananas and oranges shown below.

What fraction of the fruits he bought were oranges? Write your answer in lowest terms. Show or explain how you found your answer.

Answer _____

Quiz 24: Whole Numbers and Fractions

1   Which of these could be the number plotted on the number line?

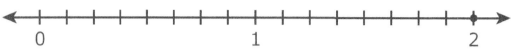

ⓐ $\frac{2}{8}$ ⓑ $\frac{8}{4}$ ⓒ $\frac{8}{2}$ ⓓ $\frac{2}{20}$

2   Which of these is plotted on the number line?

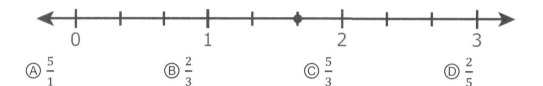

ⓐ $\frac{5}{1}$ ⓑ $\frac{2}{3}$ ⓒ $\frac{5}{3}$ ⓓ $\frac{2}{5}$

3   Which point on the number line below represents a whole number?

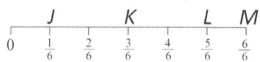

ⓐ Point *J*   ⓑ Point *K*   ⓒ Point *L*   ⓓ Point *M*

4   Which fraction does the shaded model represent?

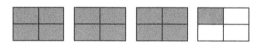

ⓐ $3\frac{3}{4}$ ⓑ $3\frac{1}{4}$ ⓒ $4\frac{3}{4}$ ⓓ $4\frac{1}{4}$

5   Which fraction does the shaded model below represent?

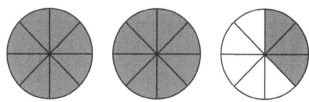

Answer _____

6   Select all the fractions below that are equal to 3.

☐ $\dfrac{2}{6}$ ☐ $\dfrac{3}{9}$ ☐ $\dfrac{1}{3}$ ☐ $\dfrac{6}{2}$

☐ $\dfrac{4}{12}$ ☐ $\dfrac{30}{10}$ ☐ $\dfrac{9}{3}$ ☐ $\dfrac{3}{3}$

7   Plot the fractions listed on the number line below.

$$\dfrac{12}{6},\ \dfrac{3}{6},\ \dfrac{6}{6},\ \dfrac{9}{6},\ \dfrac{8}{6},\ \dfrac{2}{6}$$

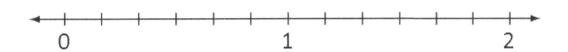

Complete each expression by writing the fraction in its simplest form.

$\dfrac{12}{6}=$ $\dfrac{3}{6}=$ $\dfrac{6}{6}=$

$\dfrac{9}{6}=$ $\dfrac{8}{6}=$ $\dfrac{2}{6}=$

8   Which fraction is equal to 8?

Ⓐ $\dfrac{1}{8}$ Ⓑ $\dfrac{8}{1}$ Ⓒ $\dfrac{8}{8}$ Ⓓ $\dfrac{8}{4}$

9   Small pies were cut into 4 equal pieces each, as shown below.

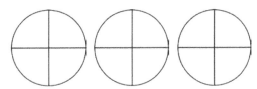

How many pieces need to be sold for 3 whole pies to be sold?

Answer _____ pieces

10   Write each fraction shown below as an improper fraction and as a mixed number. The first one has been completed for you.

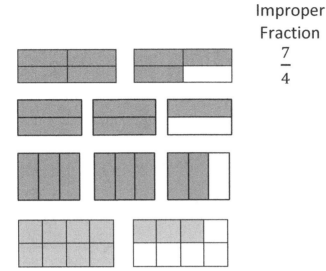

	Improper Fraction	Mixed Number
	$\dfrac{7}{4}$	$1\dfrac{3}{4}$

11   Each triangle shown below represents $\dfrac{1}{2}$ of a whole.

Which fraction is represented by the diagram below? Write your answer as an improper fraction and as a mixed number.

Answer _____ or _____

In the space below, draw triangles to represent $\dfrac{0}{2}$.

Which whole number is $\dfrac{8}{2}$ equal to? _____

12   Shade the first fraction model below to show the fraction that makes the sum equal to 1. Then complete the missing fraction in the equation.

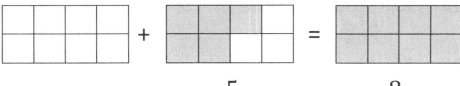

$$\frac{}{8} \quad + \quad \frac{5}{8} \quad = \quad \frac{8}{8}$$

13   Shade the diagrams below to show two fractions that add to 1. Then write an equation to show the sum of the fractions.

Equation

14   Shade the diagrams below to show three fractions that add to 1. Then write an equation to show the sum of the fractions.

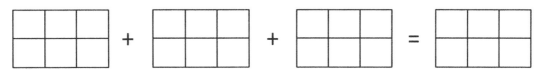

Equation

15   Shade the diagrams below to show three fractions that add to 2. Then write an equation to show the sum of the fractions.

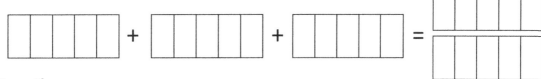

Equation

Quiz 25: Comparing Fractions

1   Which fraction below is the greatest?

Ⓐ $\frac{4}{8}$ Ⓑ $\frac{1}{4}$ Ⓒ $\frac{4}{4}$ Ⓓ $\frac{8}{4}$

2   Which set of squares has more than $\frac{3}{4}$ of the squares shaded?

3   The shaded models below represent two fractions.

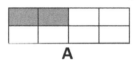   

A   **B**

What is the difference of fraction B and fraction A?

Ⓐ $\frac{5}{8}$ Ⓑ $\frac{3}{8}$ Ⓒ $\frac{1}{3}$ Ⓓ $\frac{2}{5}$

4   Place the fractions below in order from smallest to greatest. Write the numbers 1, 2, 3, and 4 on the lines to show the order.

_____ $\frac{1}{4}$

_____ $\frac{1}{8}$

_____ $\frac{3}{4}$

_____ $\frac{7}{8}$

5   Which fractions can be placed in the empty box to make the statement below true? Select all the correct answers.

$$\frac{3}{6} < \boxed{}$$

☐ $\frac{2}{6}$ ☐ $\frac{5}{6}$ ☐ $\frac{1}{3}$ ☐ $\frac{6}{6}$

☐ $\frac{1}{2}$ ☐ $\frac{2}{3}$ ☐ $\frac{1}{6}$ ☐ $\frac{4}{6}$

6   The shapes below are labeled A through G.

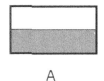 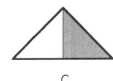

A   B   C   D   E   F   G

Which shapes have exactly $\frac{1}{2}$ the shape shaded? _____

Which shapes have less than $\frac{1}{2}$ the shape shaded? _____

Which shapes have more than $\frac{1}{2}$ the shape shaded? _____

7   Divide the rectangle below into equal areas and shade $\frac{1}{3}$ of the rectangle.

Divide the rectangle below into equal areas and shade $\frac{1}{6}$ of the rectangle.

Use the shaded models to circle the correct statement below.

$$\frac{1}{3} < \frac{1}{6} \qquad\qquad \frac{1}{3} > \frac{1}{6} \qquad\qquad \frac{1}{3} = \frac{1}{6}$$

8   Divide each square below into parts and shade the fraction listed under each.

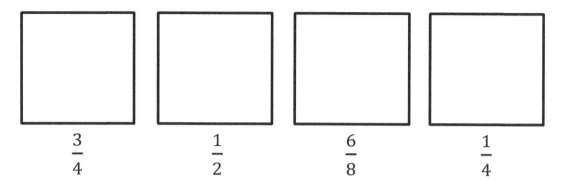

$$\frac{3}{4} \qquad \frac{1}{2} \qquad \frac{6}{8} \qquad \frac{1}{4}$$

Complete the statements below by writing the correct fractions.

The fraction ▬ is equivalent to the fraction ▬.

The fraction ▬ is twice the size of the fraction ▬.

The sum of the fractions $\frac{3}{4}$ and ▬ is equal to 1.

The fraction $\frac{3}{4}$ is 3 times the size of the fraction ▬.

9   Divide the two rectangles into equal parts and shade the fractions $\frac{2}{3}$ and $\frac{5}{6}$.

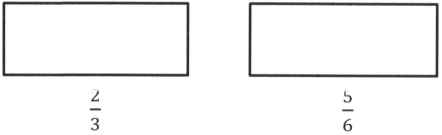

$$\frac{2}{3} \qquad\qquad \frac{5}{6}$$

Write a statement that compares the two fractions.

_____

10   Shade the models below to show $\frac{7}{10}$ and $\frac{4}{5}$.

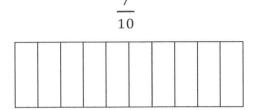

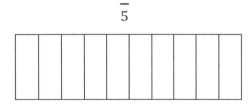

Write one of the symbols below in the number sentence to compare the fractions $\frac{7}{10}$ and $\frac{4}{5}$.

$$<, >, =$$

$\frac{7}{10}$ ☐ $\frac{4}{5}$

On the lines below, explain how the models helped you find the answer.

_____

_____

_____

11   Write a number sentence that compares the two fractions shown below. Use <, >, or = in the number sentence.

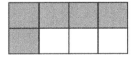   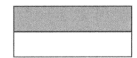

Quiz 26: Using Fractions to Solve Problems

1   The diagram below represents the lengths of yards and feet.

1 foot	1 foot	1 foot

1 yard

Based on the diagram, what fraction of 1 yard is 1 foot? _____

2   Josh buys a packet of pencils. The pencils in the packet are shown below.

What fraction of the packet is each pencil? _____

He gives 2 pencils to his friend. What fraction of the pencils does he give to his friend? _____

He divides the remaining pencils into equal halves. How many pencils are in each half? _____

3   How many $\frac{1}{4}$ cup serves of juice can be made from 2 cups of juice?

Answer _____ serves

4   The diagram represents a parking lot that is $\frac{1}{3}$ full. How many more cars need to park for it to be $\frac{1}{2}$ full?

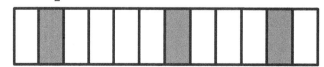

Answer _____ cars

5   The 6 guests at a party each ate 1 equal slice of cake. In all, the guests ate 1 whole cake. Complete the diagram to show one way the cake could have been divided.

6   Alex made the graph below to show how long he spent studying each subject one week.

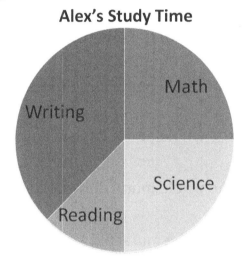

Which subject did Alex study for $\frac{1}{8}$ of his study time? _____

What fraction of his study time was spent studying math? _____

Alex studied science for 30 minutes. How long did he study math, reading, and writing for? Show your work or explain how you found your answer.

Math _____ minutes **Reading** _____ minutes **Writing** _____ minutes

7   A group of students divided a mural into equal parts. The diagram below shows who painted each part of the mural.

Leo	Leo	Jane	Jane	Jane	Jane
Leo	Abby	Abby	Lisa	Ryan	Ryan

Which student painted $\frac{1}{3}$ of the mural? _____

What fraction of the whole mural did Abby paint? _____

What fraction of the whole mural did Lisa and Ryan paint in all? _____

What fraction of the whole mural did Jane and Ryan paint in all? _____

What fraction more of the mural did Jane paint than Ryan? Show or explain how you found your answer.

Answer _____

If equal parts of the mural were painted by 6 students, what fraction would each students paint? Show or explain how you found your answer.

Answer _____

8   Trey made the chart below to show how many three-point shots he made and missing during the first half of the basketball season.

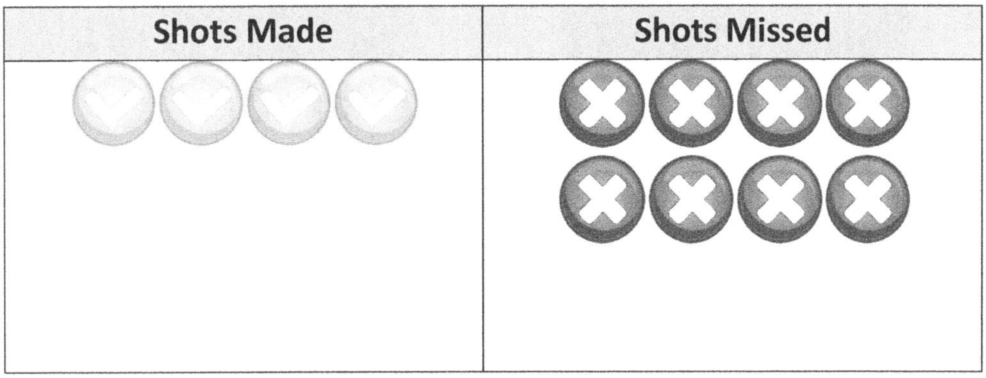

Shots Made	Shots Missed

What fraction of his total shots did Trey make? Show or explain how you found your answer.

Answer _____

In the second half of the season, Trey had 12 attempts. He ends the year with $\frac{1}{2}$ his total shots made and $\frac{1}{2}$ his total shots missed. How many shots did he make and how many did he miss in the second half of the season? Show or explain how you found your answer.

Answer _____ shots made, _____ shots missed

Quizzes 27 to 40

Measurement

Directions

Read each question carefully. For each multiple-choice question, fill in the circle for the correct answer. For other types of questions, follow the directions given in the question.

You may use a ruler to help you answer questions. You should answer the questions without using a calculator.

COMMON CORE SKILLS LIST
For Parents, Teachers, and Tutors

Quizzes 27 through 40 cover these skills from the Common Core State Standards.

Measurement

Solve problems involving measurement and estimation of intervals of time, liquid volumes, and masses of objects.
1. Tell and write time to the nearest minute and measure time intervals in minutes. Solve word problems involving addition and subtraction of time intervals in minutes.
2. Measure and estimate liquid volumes and masses of objects using standard units of grams (g), kilograms (kg), and liters (l). Add, subtract, multiply, or divide to solve one-step word problems involving masses or volumes that are given in the same units.

Geometric measurement: understand concepts of area and relate area to multiplication and to addition.
5. Recognize area as an attribute of plane figures and understand concepts of area measurement.
6. Measure areas by counting unit squares.
7. Relate area to the operations of multiplication and addition.
> a. Find the area of a rectangle with whole-number side lengths by tiling it, and show that the area is the same as would be found by multiplying the side lengths.
> b. Multiply side lengths to find areas of rectangles with whole-number side lengths in the context of solving real world and mathematical problems, and represent whole-number products as rectangular areas in mathematical reasoning.
> c. Use tiling to show in a concrete case that the area of a rectangle with whole-number side lengths a and $b + c$ is the sum of $a \times b$ and $a \times c$. Use area models to represent the distributive property in mathematical reasoning.
> d. Recognize area as additive. Find areas of rectilinear figures by decomposing them into non-overlapping rectangles and adding the areas of the non-overlapping parts, applying this technique to solve real world problems.

Geometric measurement: recognize perimeter as an attribute of plane figures and distinguish between linear and area measures.
8. Solve real world and mathematical problems involving perimeters of polygons, including finding the perimeter given the side lengths, finding an unknown side length, and exhibiting rectangles with the same perimeter and different areas or with the same area and different perimeters.

Quiz 27: Writing and Measuring Time

1   What time is shown on the clock below?

Ⓐ 11:10   Ⓑ 1:55   Ⓒ 11:02   Ⓓ 2:05

2   Which of the following is closest to the time shown on the clock?

Ⓐ 6:20   Ⓑ 4:30   Ⓒ 4:45   Ⓓ 9:00

3   Which of these is one way to write the time shown on the clock below?

Ⓐ quarter past one   Ⓑ ten past one

Ⓒ five past three   Ⓓ three fifteen

4   Harriet said she had a meeting at twenty to two in the afternoon. Which of these shows the time of the meeting?

Ⓐ 1:40 a.m.   Ⓑ 1:40 p.m.   Ⓒ 2:20 a.m.   Ⓓ 2:20 p.m.

5   Write the times listed below in number form.

quarter past one   _____ : _____   ten to eleven   _____ : _____

half past ten   _____ : _____   quarter to nine   _____ : _____

five to seven   _____ : _____   ten past five   _____ : _____

twenty past six   _____ : _____   five past twelve   _____ : _____

6   Write the time shown on each clock on the line below it.

_____   _____   _____   _____   _____

7   Write the time shown on each clock to the nearest minute.

_____ : _____   _____ : _____   _____ : _____   _____ : _____

_____ : _____   _____ : _____   _____ : _____   _____ : _____

Quiz 28: Adding and Subtracting Time

1   David started reading at the time shown on the clock below.

He read for 42 minutes. What time did he finish reading?

Ⓐ 2:47   Ⓑ 3:07   Ⓒ 5:54   Ⓓ 6:04

2   Carly is meeting a friend at the library at 4:15 p.m. It takes Carly 25 minutes to walk to the library. She wants to arrive 5 minutes early. What time should she leave?

Ⓐ 3:25 p.m.   Ⓑ 3:35 p.m.   Ⓒ 3:45 p.m.   Ⓓ 3:55 p.m.

3   Sawyer started riding to school at 8:45 a.m. It took him 35 minutes to get to school. What time did he get to school?

Ⓐ 9:00 a.m.   Ⓑ 9:10 a.m.   Ⓒ 9:15 a.m.   Ⓓ 9:20 a.m.

4   Ricky started a guitar lesson at 3:40 p.m. The lesson finished at 5:05 p.m. How long did the guitar lesson go for?

Ⓐ 25 min   Ⓑ 55 min   Ⓒ 1 hr 25 min   Ⓓ 1 hr 55 min

5   Hannah's flight was meant to leave at 12:42 p.m. The flight left at 1:06 p.m. How many minutes late was the flight?

Ⓐ 12 minutes   Ⓑ 18 minutes   Ⓒ 22 minutes   Ⓓ 24 minutes

6   Bianca put a pie in the oven at 5:05 and baked it for 85 minutes. She let it cool for 25 minutes, and then served it. What time did she serve it?

Ⓐ 6:30   Ⓑ 6:40   Ⓒ 6:50   Ⓓ 7:00

7   Noah recorded the start and end time of the phone calls he made. Which phone calls went for more than 15 minutes? Select all the correct answers.

☐ 8:54 a.m. to 9:08 a.m.   ☐ 9:12 a.m. to 9:23 a.m.

☐ 7:03 p.m. to 7:20 p.m.   ☐ 11:48 a.m. to 12:01 p.m.

☐ 5:16 p.m. to 5:35 p.m.   ☐ 10:57 p.m. to 11:14 p.m.

8   The table below shows the start and end time of six movies. Complete the table by writing the length of each movie in hours and minutes.

Start Time	End Time	Length
9:45 a.m.	11:20 a.m.	
10:15 a.m.	12:10 p.m.	
11:20 a.m.	12:55 p.m.	
12:05 p.m.	2:30 p.m.	
1:35 p.m.	3:15 p.m.	
3:50 p.m.	5:40 p.m.	

9   The clocks show the time Jack started and finished work one evening.

Start   End

What time did Jack work from? _____ to _____

How long did Jack work for? _____ hours, _____ minutes

Jack got home 40 minutes after work ended. What time did he get home?

_____

10   Thomas drove to visit his uncle. He left home in the evening at the time shown on the first clock. He arrived at his uncle's house in the evening at the time shown on the second clock. How long did Thomas drive for?

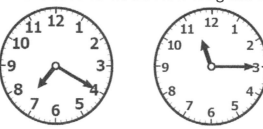

Answer _____ hours, _____ minutes

11   Kobe got on a train at 1:45 p.m. He got off the train at 4:15 p.m. On the number line, plot the points to show when Kobe got on and off the train.

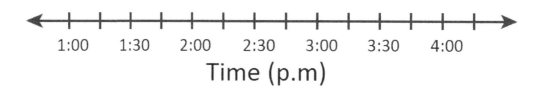

Time (p.m)

How long was Kobe on the train for? _____ hours, _____ minutes

12   Mia arrived at her restaurant job at 6:00 p.m. She worked for 1 hour and 30 minutes. Then she took a break of 15 minutes. She worked for another 1 hour and 45 minutes. Plot the following points on the number line below. Use the letter given to mark each point.

A – the time Mia started   **B** – the time Mia's break started
C – the time Mia's break ended   **D** – the time Mia finished work

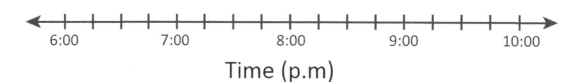

Time (p.m)

How long did Mia work for, including her break? _____ hours, _____ minutes

13   Students competed in a cycling race one morning. To avoid accidents, pairs of students started the race at different times. The table shows the results of the race. Complete the table with the missing information.

Student	Start Time	End Time	Total Time
Leyton	8:05	9:42	
Matt	8:05		1 hour 42 minutes
Omar	8:20		1 hour 35 minutes
Sean	8:20	9:48	
Perry	8:35	10:18	
Tim	8:35		1 hour 26 minutes
Sonny	8:50	10:39	
Ruben	8:50		1 hour 31 minutes

Who took the least time to finish the race? _____

Who took the most time to finish the race? _____

14   The table below shows a coach's plan for a basketball training session.

Task	Warm-up	Passing Practice	Dribbling Practice	Shooting Practice	Practice Game
Time (min)	5	14	12	18	45

The training session starts at 6:00 p.m. and ends at 7:40 p.m. How much time will be left over?

Show your work.

Answer _____ minutes

Quiz 29: Measuring and Estimating Liquid Volume

1   What is the most likely volume of the cooking pot shown below?

Ⓐ 5 liters   Ⓑ 50 liters   Ⓒ 500 liters   Ⓓ 5,000 liters

2   A store has the four fish tanks shown below for sale. Adam buys the tank with the greatest volume. Which tank did Adam buy?

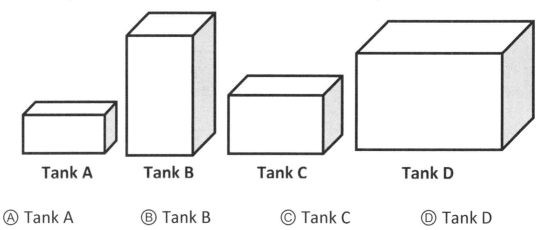

Tank A   Tank B   Tank C   Tank D

Ⓐ Tank A   Ⓑ Tank B   Ⓒ Tank C   Ⓓ Tank D

3   A 1-liter jug is filled with orange juice to the line shown.

How much orange juice is in the jug?

Ⓐ $\frac{1}{4}$ liter   Ⓑ $\frac{1}{2}$ liter   Ⓒ 2 liters   Ⓓ 4 liters

4   Sara filled the container below with water.

To the nearest liter, how much water did she fill the container with?

Answer _____ liters

5   Write the volume of water in each container on the line below it.

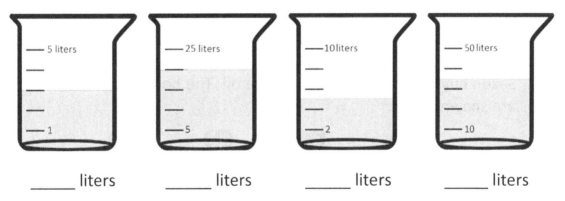

_____ liters   _____ liters   _____ liters   _____ liters

6   A 100 ml beaker is filled to the line below. The 150 ml and 250 ml beakers are then filled with the same amount of water. Draw lines to show the volume of water in the 150 ml and 250 ml beakers.

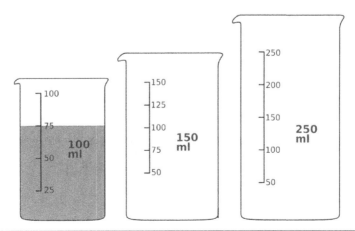

Quiz 30: Solving Word Problems Involving Liquid Volume

1   Jayden and Alana each have containers the same size, filled with different amounts of water.

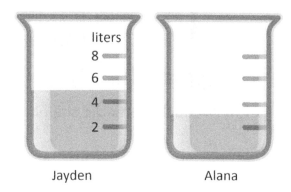

How much water is in Alana's container?

Ⓐ 2 liters   Ⓑ 3 liters   Ⓒ 4 liters   Ⓓ 5 liters

2   Saxon buys a total of 2 liters of olive oil. The bottles of olive oil he bought are shown below.

How much olive oil is in each bottle?

Ⓐ $\frac{1}{1}$ liter   Ⓑ $\frac{1}{2}$ liter   Ⓒ 4 liters   Ⓓ 8 liters

3   Anthony is filling a fish tank with water. He fills a 4-liter bucket with water and adds it to the tank. He does this a total of 6 times until the tank is full. How much water is in the tank when it is full?

Ⓐ 10 liters   Ⓑ 24 liters   Ⓒ 32 liters   Ⓓ 60 liters

4   Donna was measuring out the ingredients for a cake. The diagram below shows the amount of milk and cream she needs.

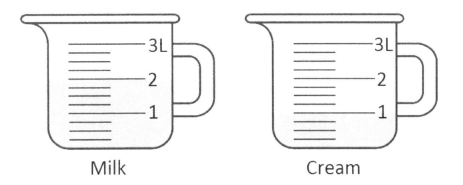

How much more milk than cream does she need? _____

How much milk and cream does she need in all? _____

5   The diagram below shows the volume of soil garden beds of different sizes can hold.

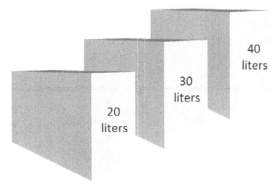

Don buys 5 bags of soil containing 20 liters of soil each. How much soil will Don have left after he fills all three garden beds?

Show your work.

Answer _____ liters

6   A baker fills 8 measuring cups with 1 liter of plain flour each, as shown below.

The baker needs $\frac{1}{2}$ liter of plain flour to make each loaf of bread. How many loaves of bread can the baker make?

Show your work.

Answer _____ loaves

7   The diagram below shows the amount of water a farmer has in four different tanks.

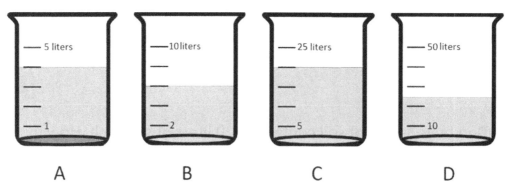

How much water is in all the tanks combined?

Show your work.

Answer _____ liters

8   Erika had the two beakers of water shown below. She poured all the water into the third beaker. Draw a line to show the volume of water in the third beaker.

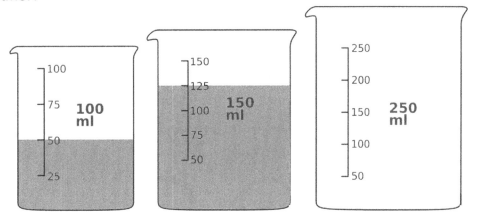

How much water is in the third beaker? _____ milliliters

She wants to pour all the water back into the first beaker. Is this possible? Explain why or why not.

_____

_____

_____

9   A full jug of grain is poured into a box and fills the box completely. What does this show about the volume of the jug and the box?

_____

_____

_____

Quiz 31: Measuring and Estimating Mass

1   What is the most likely mass of a paperclip?

Ⓐ 1 gram   Ⓑ 100 grams   Ⓒ 1 kilogram   Ⓓ 100 kilograms

2   What is the most likely mass of the bicycle shown below?

Ⓐ 1 g   Ⓑ 100 g   Ⓒ 10 kg   Ⓓ 1000 kg

3   Which item in a kitchen is most likely to have a mass close to 10 grams?

Ⓐ teaspoon   Ⓑ toaster   Ⓒ frying pan   Ⓓ dinner plate

4   Match each item listed below to its most likely mass. Draw lines to connect the items.

strawberry   1 gram

olive   1 kilogram

watermelon   100 grams

banana   10 grams

5   For a school project, the students weighed items in the classroom. For each item listed below, select the correct unit of either grams or kilograms. Write kg or g on the blank line to show your choice.

Item	Mass
stapler	300 ___
desk	15 ___
pencil	40 ___
laptop	2 ___
whiteboard	12 ___
ruler	60 ___

6   When apples are placed on a scale, the scale has the reading shown.

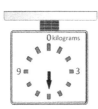

What is the mass of the apples? _____ kilograms

7   What reading is shown on the scale below? Write the answer in grams and kilograms.

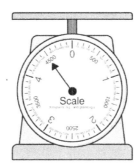

Answer _____ grams or _____ kilograms

Quiz 32: Solving Word Problems Involving Mass

1   A weightlifter places a 20 kilogram, 10 kilogram, and 5 kilogram weight on each end of a bar.

What is the total mass of the weights added to the bar?

Ⓐ 35 kg   Ⓑ 45 kg   Ⓒ 60 kg   Ⓓ 70 kg

2   Soil is sold for $4 for each 10 kilogram bag. Rhys uses 60 kilograms of soil to fill the small garden. He uses twice as much soil to fill the large garden.

How much would it cost to fill the large garden with soil?

Ⓐ $24   Ⓑ $48   Ⓒ $60   Ⓓ $120

3   The diagram shows that a scale is balanced when a large notebook is placed on one side, and two small notebooks are placed on the other side.

If the large notebook has a mass of 800 grams, which of these could be the masses of the small notebooks? Select all the possible answers.

☐ 200 grams and 600 grams   ☐ 500 grams and 500 grams

☐ 750 grams and 250 grams   ☐ 300 grams and 300 grams

☐ 400 grams and 400 grams   ☐ 450 grams and 550 grams

4   What is the total mass of the weights shown below?

Answer _____ kilograms

5   An empty delivery van has a mass of 2,800 kilograms. After being loaded with 20 televisions of equal mass, the total mass is 3,100 kilograms. What is the mass of each television?

Show your work.

Answer _____ kilograms

6   Jenna made jars of strawberry jelly with the same mass. She placed three jars on a scale, as shown below.

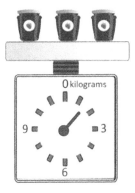

How many jars will have a total mass of 6 kilograms?

Show your work.

Answer _____ jars

7   Tina weighs her bags before going to the airport. The mass of the bags is shown below.

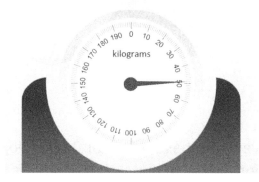

What is the mass of the bags to the nearest kilogram? _____ kg

The fee for luggage is free for the first 30 kilograms and $10 for each kilogram over 30 kilograms. How much will Tina be charged for her luggage?

Show your work.

Answer $_____

8   Nathan drew the diagram below to show what happened when he placed 2 apples on one end of a scale and 3 oranges on the other end.

Nathan states that each orange must weigh more than each apple. Explain why this may not be correct.

_____

_____

_____

9   Three students collected rocks and weighed the rocks they collected. The diagram below shows the mass of each student's rocks.

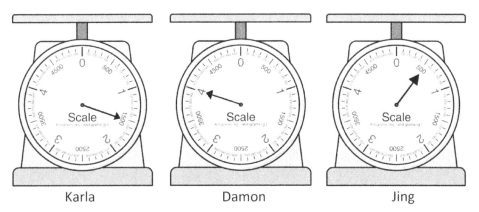

Karla	Damon	Jing

Which student's rocks had the lowest mass? _____

What was the mass of Damon's rocks? _____ kilograms

How much greater was the mass of Karla's rocks than Jing's?

Show your work.

Answer _____ grams

What is the total mass of all the rocks?

Show your work.

Answer _____ kilograms or _____ grams

Damon says that his rocks have twice the mass of Karla and Jing's rocks combined. Explain whether or not Damon is correct and tell why.

_____

_____

_____

Quiz 33: Understanding Area

1   Justine makes some statements about the top of a table. Which statement describes the area of the top of the table?

Ⓐ It would take 24 inches of tape to place a border around it.

Ⓑ It would take 18 square-inch tiles to cover it.

Ⓒ It is 9 inches from one side to the other.

Ⓓ It is 30 inches above the ground.

2   Which question can be answered by finding the area of the football field?

Ⓐ How many steps would need to be taken to walk around the edge of the football field once?

Ⓑ How long would it take to walk from one end of the field to the other?

Ⓒ How many 1-meter square sheets would it take to cover the football field completely?

Ⓓ How many 1-meter rulers could be laid from the left side of the field to the right?

3   Zane wants to find the area of a poster. Which two details does Zane need to find the area? Select the two correct answers.

☐ how much it cost   ☐ how wide it is

☐ how tall it is   ☐ how heavy it is

4   Skye uses 1-inch squares to make a rectangle. She uses 12 squares. Which of these can be determined from this? Select all the correct answers.

☐ the length of the rectangle   ☐ the height of the rectangle

☐ the area of the rectangle   ☐ the perimeter of the rectangle

5   The picture below shows six photo frames labeled A through F.

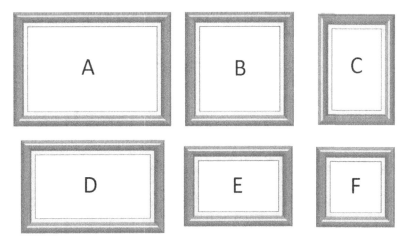

Which frame appears to have the greatest area? _____

Which frame appears to have the smallest area? _____

Which two frames appear to have the same area? _____ and _____

Explain how you could check your answers.

_____

_____

_____

6   A banner is divided into 4 rows of 9 squares each. Each square has an area of 1 square foot.

What is the area of the banner?

Answer _____ square feet

7   Kendra has a piece of note paper that is 6 inches long and 2 inches wide. She cut it into squares of 1 square inch each. Draw lines below to show how she cut the note paper.

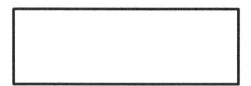

How many squares did she cut the note paper into? _____

Explain what this tells you about the area of the note paper.

_____

_____

_____

8   The grids below have squares with units of 1 square centimeter (cm^2). Draw a rectangle on the first grid with the length, height, and area given. Then draw rectangles on the second and third grids to match the information given, and complete the missing information.

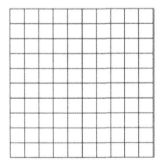   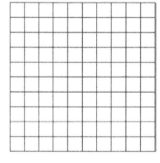   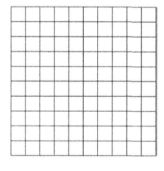

Length = 4 cm   Length = 8 cm   Length = ____ cm
Height = 6 cm   Height = ____ cm   Height = 3 cm
Area = 24 cm^2 Area = 40 cm^2 Area = 27 cm^2

9   Two vegetable gardens are shaped like rectangles. The small garden is 6 feet long and 3 feet wide. The large garden is also 3 feet wide, but is 12 feet long.

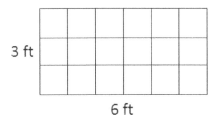

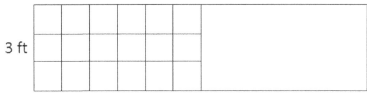

What is the area of the small garden? _____ square feet

How can the area of the small garden be used to find the area of the large garden? Explain your answer.

_____

_____

_____

A third garden has the same area as the large garden, but is shaped like a square. What are the side lengths of the third garden?

Show your work.

Answer _____ feet

Quiz 34: Measuring Area by Counting

1   Each square on the grid below measures 1 cm by 1 cm. What is the area of the shaded figure on the grid?

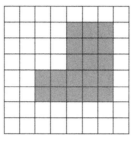

    Ⓐ 17 cm²   Ⓑ 18 cm²   Ⓒ 19 cm²   Ⓓ 20 cm²

2   Joseph made the design below on grid paper. What is the area of the shaded part of Joseph's design, in square units?

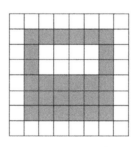

    Ⓐ 24   Ⓑ 28   Ⓒ 30   Ⓓ 36

3   Each square on the grid below measures 1 cm by 1 cm.

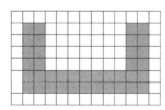

Which expressions can be used to find the area of the shaded shape, in square centimeters? Select all the correct answers.

☐ 12 + 14 + 12   ☐ 8 + 14 + 8

☐ 12 + 22 + 8   ☐ 8 + 22 + 8

4   Find the area of each figure shown below. Write the area on the blank line.

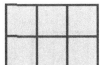 = one square inch

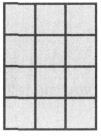

____ square inches   ____ square inches   ____ square inches

____ square inches   ____ square inches   ____ square inches

5   The shapes below are each made out of 1 unit squares. Find the area of each shape in square units. Write each area on the line under each shape.

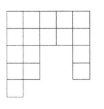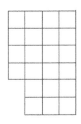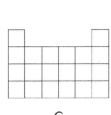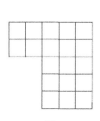

A   B   C   D   E

_____   _____   _____   _____   _____

Identify the shape whose area can be found by each expression below. Write the letter for the correct shape on the blank line.

____ (6 × 3) + 1 + 1   ____ (3 × 2) + (2 × 2) + (3 × 2)

____ (4 × 6) - 2   ____ 5 + 5 + 3 + 3 + 3

6   A rectangular garden has an area of 18 square meters. The garden is 6 meters long. Draw the shape of the garden on the grid below.

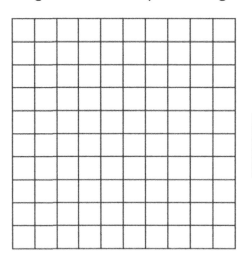

KEY

☐ = 1 square meter

Complete the number sentences below to show two ways you can tell that the area of the garden is 18 square meters.

_____ × _____ = 18   _____ + _____ + _____ = 18

7   Carly drew the shape below on a grid.

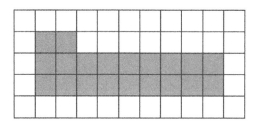

Complete the addition expression that can be used to find the area of the shape, in square units.

(3 × 2) + (_____ × _____)

Complete the subtraction expression that can be used to find the area of the shape.

(3 × 9) - (_____ × _____)

8   The shaded part of the diagram below represents the part of a park that is used for a playground. Each square represents 1 square meter.

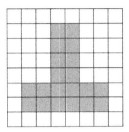

What is the area of the playground? Use words or equations to show how you found your answer.

Answer _____ square meters

What is the area of the park that is not used for a playground? Use words or equations to show how you found your answer.

Answer _____ square meters

9   Dom drew two shapes on a grid, as shown below.

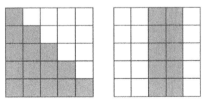

How many more square units is the first shape than the second shape? Use words or equations to show how you found your answer.

Answer _____ square units

Quiz 35: Finding the Area of a Rectangle

1   A rectangular poster is 6 inches wide and 8 inches high. What is the area of the poster?

Ⓐ 14 square inches   Ⓑ 28 square inches

Ⓒ 42 square inches   Ⓓ 48 square inches

2   Kyle's bedroom floor is in the shape of a rectangle. It is 8 feet long and 9 feet wide. What is the area of Kyle's bedroom floor?

Ⓐ 17 square feet   Ⓑ 34 square feet

Ⓒ 72 square feet   Ⓓ 89 square feet

3   Which expression can be used to find the area of a rectangle with a length of 3 meters and a width of 7 meters, in square meters?

Ⓐ 3 + 7   Ⓑ 3 × 7

Ⓒ 2 × (3 + 7)   Ⓓ 3 × 3 × 3

4   What is the area of the rectangle shown below?

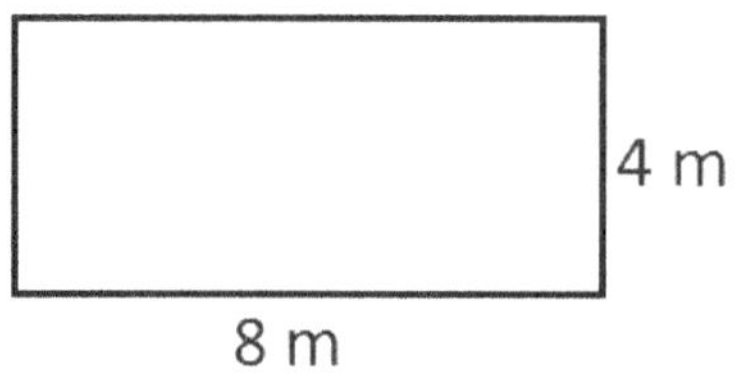

8 m

4 m

Answer _____ square meters

5   Em has 1-inch square stickers. She uses exactly 36 square stickers to cover the front of a book. There are no gaps and no overlaps. Which of these could be the measurements of the cover? Select all the possible answers.

☐ 4 inch by 9 inch   ☐ 8 inch by 7 inch   ☐ 6 inch by 6 inch

☐ 5 inch by 6 inch   ☐ 12 inch by 3 inch   ☐ 16 inch by 2 inch

6   The table below shows the length, width, and area of different rectangular fields. Complete the table with the missing information.

Length (meters)	Width (meters)	Area (square meters)
5	7	
10		40
	9	27
3		15
6		42
	2	40
30		90

7   The rectangle below has an area of 56 square inches.

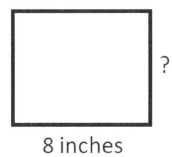

8 inches

What is the length of the missing side? Show or explain how you got your answer.

Answer _____ inches

8   Jackson shaded 24 squares on a grid to create a rectangle. On the grids below, shade the four possible rectangles Jackson could have shaded. Write the possible lengths and heights under each grid.

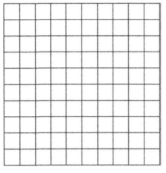

Length _____ units
Height _____ units

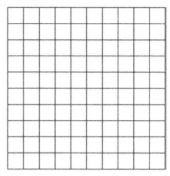

Length _____ units
Height _____ units

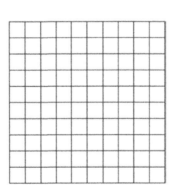

Length _____ units
Height _____ units

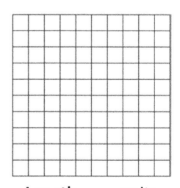

Length _____ units
Height _____ units

9   The shaded area on the grid represents a shape with an area of 12 square units. Complete the equation that shows that the area is 12 square units. Then draw a shape on the second grid with a different length but the same area. Complete the equation to show that the area is the same.

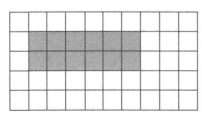 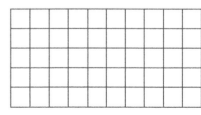

_____ × _____ = _____   _____ × _____ = _____

10   Find the area of each rectangle shown below.

A _____ square feet   **B** _____ square feet   **C** _____ square feet

Explain how you can tell that the sum of the areas of rectangles B and C will be equal to the area of rectangle A.

_____

_____

_____

11   Sofia is making a quilt out of 1-inch squares. The quilt will be 8 squares long, as shown below.

Sofia wants the quilt to have a total area of 32 square inches. How many squares wide must the quilt be? Show or explain how you got your answer.

Answer _____ squares

Quiz 36: Using Multiplication to Find Area

1 A rectangle has a length of 4 inches and a width of 3 inches. Which expression can be used to find the area of the rectangle, in square inches?

Ⓐ 2 × (3 + 4)   Ⓑ 4 × 3 × 2   Ⓒ 4 × 3   Ⓓ 4 × 4 × 3 × 3

2 A laptop screen is 12 inches wide and 9 inches high. Which expression could **NOT** be used to find the area of the screen, in square inches?

Ⓐ 12 × 9   Ⓑ 9 + 9 + 9 + 9 + 9 + 9 + 9 + 9 + 9

Ⓒ 9 × 12   Ⓓ 12 + 12 + 12 + 12 + 12 + 12 + 12 + 12 + 12

3 Lu has a rectangular garden with an area of 24 square feet. Which of these could be the measurements of the garden? Select all the possible answers.

☐ 8 feet by 3 feet   ☐ 12 feet by 12 feet

☐ 2 feet by 3 feet   ☐ 4 feet by 6 feet

☐ 5 feet by 8 feet   ☐ 5 feet by 5 feet

☐ 12 feet by 2 feet   ☐ 8 feet by 4 feet

4 A square rug has an area of 16 square meters. Draw the rug on the grid.

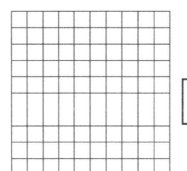

KEY
☐ = 1 square meter

Complete the number sentence below that shows how to find the area of the rug, in square meters.

_____ × _____ = 16

5   Maria is making a quilt by sewing together 1-foot squares of material. Maria has 50 1-foot squares. Maria wants to choose a size that will use exactly 50 squares. What size could Maria make the quilt? Show or explain how you got your answer.

Answer _____ feet long and _____ feet wide

If Maria decides to make a square quilt with 50 squares or less, what is the greatest side length Maria could use? Show or explain how you got your answer.

Answer _____ feet

Maria wants the quilt to be 12 feet long and 6 feet wide. How many more 1-foot squares does Maria need? Show or explain how you got your answer.

Answer _____ squares

6   The rectangle below is divided into two equal rectangles, as shown.

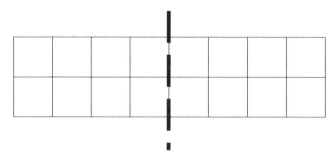

Complete the equations below to show that the area of the large rectangle is equal to the sum of the areas of the two smaller rectangles.

_____ × _____ = _____

(_____ × _____) + (_____ × _____) = _____

7   The diagram below shows one large rectangle and two smaller rectangles.

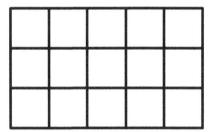 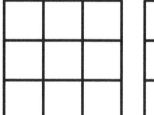 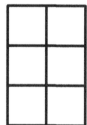

How can you tell that the area of the large rectangle is equal to the sum of the areas of the two smaller rectangles? Use words, diagrams, or equations to explain your answer.

8   Erin is making a design out of tiles by gluing 1-inch square tiles onto a wooden board. She has the tiles listed below.

     14 blue tiles
     10 red tiles
     16 green tiles

She glues the tiles onto the board in a rectangular shape with no gaps between the tiles. What is the area of the design she makes?

Show your work.

Answer _____ square inches

Erin decides she wants 8 tiles in each row. Write an equation that can be used to find how many rows of tiles she can place.

Equation

On the grid below, draw another rectangular shape Erin could make using all the tiles. Then write an equation to show how to find the area of the shape.

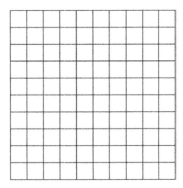

Equation

Quiz 37: Finding the Area of Complex Shapes

1   Which of these finds the area of the shape below, in square units?

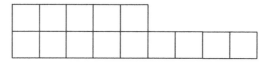

   Ⓐ (2 × 2) + 4 = 8   Ⓑ (2 × 4) + 5 = 13

   Ⓒ (5 × 2) + 4 = 14   Ⓓ (5 × 4) + 5 = 25

2   What is the area of the shaded figure on the grid, in square units?

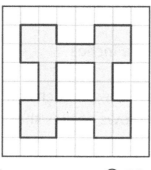

  Ⓐ 20   Ⓑ 24   Ⓒ 28   Ⓓ 32

3   Allison made a shape by placing two pieces of cardboard together, as shown below.

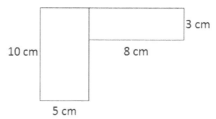

She adds a third piece of cardboard to make a shape with a total area of 130 square centimeters. Which of these could be the shape of the third piece of cardboard?

   Ⓐ 5 cm by 10 cm   Ⓑ 3 cm by 13 cm

   Ⓒ 8 cm by 7 cm   Ⓓ 6 cm by 9 cm

4   Complete the expressions to show how to find the area of each shape, in square units.

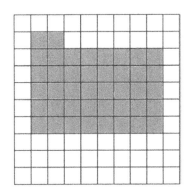

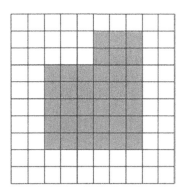

(___ × ___) + (___ × ___)   (___ × ___) + (___ × ___)

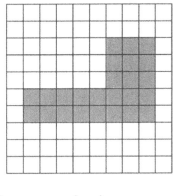

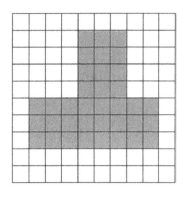

(___ × ___) + (___ × ___)   (___ × ___) + (___ × ___)

5   Draw a shape on each grid whose area can be found by the calculation shown.

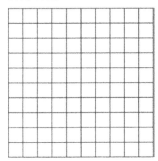

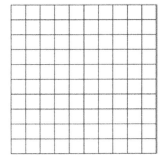

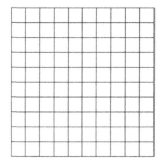

(6 × 2) + (4 × 3) = 24   (5 × 2) + (3 × 3) = 19   (8 × 1) + (2 × 4) = 16

6   Sally used the expression (5 × 4) + (8 × 2) to find the area of a kitchen bench, in square feet. On the grid below, draw one possible shape of the kitchen bench. Then find the area of the kitchen bench.

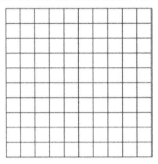

Answer _____ square feet

7   The diagram below shows the shape of George's kitchen floor.

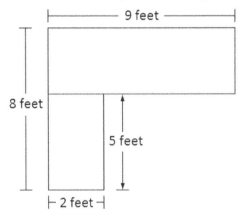

George wants to tile the kitchen floor with 1-foot square tiles. Each tile costs $3. What is the total cost of the tiles George needs?

Show your work.

Answer $_____

8   A model of the shape of a swimming pool is shown below. A fence is built around the pool 2 meters from each edge.

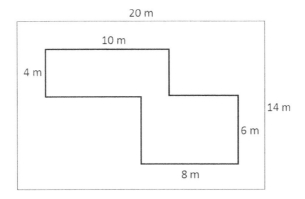

What is the area of the base of the swimming pool? Use words or equations to show how you found your answer.

Answer _____ square meters

The area around the pool inside the fence is tiled. What is the area of the tiled area? Use words or equations to show how you found your answer.

Answer _____ square meters

9   Kieran covered the top of a desk with wooden panels, as shown below.

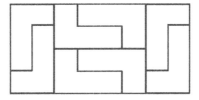

Each panel had an area of 4 square feet. What is the total area covered by the panels? Show or explain how you found your answer.

Answer _____ square feet

Quiz 38: Understanding and Measuring Perimeter

1   Which question can be answered by finding the perimeter of a paddock?

    Ⓐ How many cows can be placed in the paddock if each cow needs a space of 100 square feet?

    Ⓑ What is the total length of fencing needed to go around all the edges of the paddock once?

    Ⓒ How many fields of 1 square yard each can the paddock be divided into?

    Ⓓ How many 1-yard rulers could be laid in a straight line from the left side of the paddock to the right?

2   A picture frame is 8 inches wide and 5 inches high. What is the perimeter of the frame?

    Ⓐ 26 inches   Ⓑ 32 inches   Ⓒ 20 inches   Ⓓ 40 inches

3   What is the perimeter of the rectangle shown below?

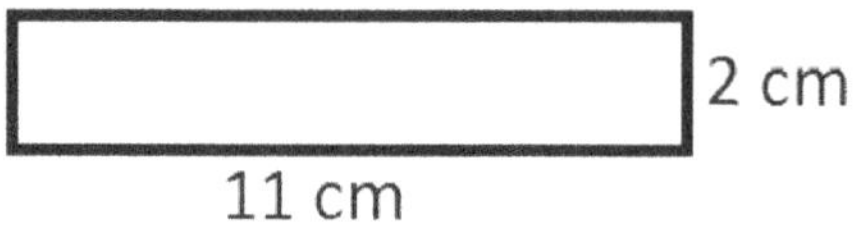

2 cm

11 cm

    Ⓐ 13 cm   Ⓑ 18 cm   Ⓒ 22 cm   Ⓓ 26 cm

4   The dimensions of different rectangles are listed below. Select all the rectangles that have the same perimeters.

    ☐ 7 cm by 3 cm   ☐ 10 cm by 2 cm   ☐ 5 cm by 12 cm

    ☐ 4 cm by 9 cm   ☐ 9 cm by 1 cm   ☐ 8 cm by 2 cm

    ☐ 15 cm by 3 cm   ☐ 4 cm by 5 cm   ☐ 6 cm by 9 cm

    ☐ 8 cm by 6 cm   ☐ 6 cm by 4 cm   ☐ 3 cm by 8 cm

5   Each grid has squares of 1 cm by 1 cm. For each shaded shape, complete the number sentence that can be used to find the perimeter of the shape. Then complete the calculation to find the perimeter.

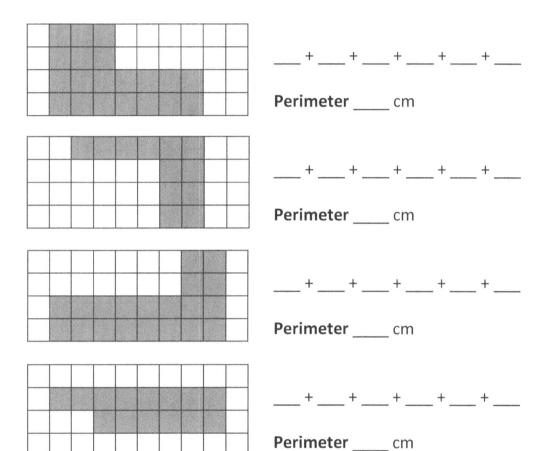

____ + ____ + ____ + ____ + ____ + ____

Perimeter _____ cm

____ + ____ + ____ + ____ + ____ + ____

Perimeter _____ cm

____ + ____ + ____ + ____ + ____ + ____

Perimeter _____ cm

____ + ____ + ____ + ____ + ____ + ____

Perimeter _____ cm

6   Frankie used 1-inch square cards to make the rectangles shown below. Complete the equations to show two different ways to find the perimeter of each rectangle, in inches.

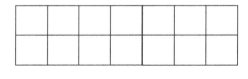

2 x (_____ + _____) = _____

_____ + _____ + _____ + _____ = _____

2 x (_____ + _____) = _____

_____ + _____ + _____ + _____ = _____

7   A block for a children's puzzle has the shape shown below.

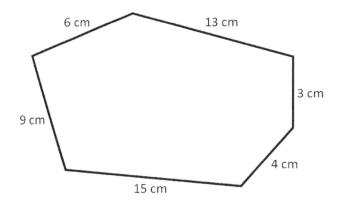

What is the perimeter of the block?

Show your work.

Answer _____ cm

8   Joel used cubes with side lengths of 1 inch to build a border around a garden bed, as shown below.

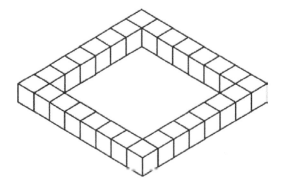

What is the perimeter of the outside of the garden bed? Show your work or explain how you found your answer.

Answer _____ inches

9   The grids below have squares with side lengths of 1 cm. Draw a rectangle
on the first grid with the length and height given. Then find the perimeter
of the rectangle. Draw rectangles on the second and third grids to match
the information given, and complete the missing information.

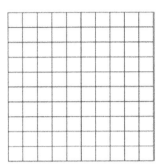 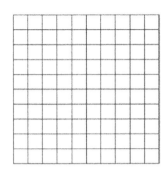 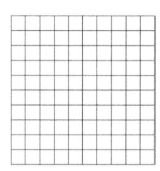

Length = 8 cm   Length = 10 cm   Length = _____ cm
Height = 3 cm   Height = _____ cm   Height = 7 cm
Perimeter = _____ cm   Perimeter = 32 cm   Perimeter = 26 cm

10   Lexie wants to cut out a rectangular note card. She wants the card to have
a perimeter of 24 cm. Draw two possible dimensions of Lexie's card on the
1-centimeter grids below. Then write equations to show that the
perimeter of each is 24 cm.

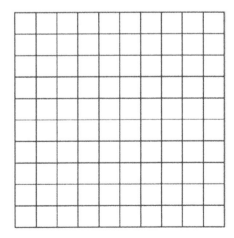   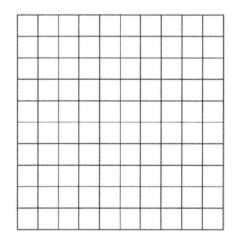

Equation   **Equation**

Quiz 39: Solving Problems Involving Perimeter

1 The rectangle below has a perimeter of 28 cm.

4 cm

? cm

What is the length of the rectangle?

Ⓐ 7 cm   Ⓑ 10 cm   Ⓒ 12 cm   Ⓓ 20 cm

2 Priya has 40 feet of logs she can place around the four sides of a rectangular garden bed. She wants the garden bed to be 8 feet long. How wide should the garden be to use all the logs?

Ⓐ 5 feet   Ⓑ 6 feet   Ⓒ 12 feet   Ⓓ 16 feet

3 Max and his classmates are making signs to hang around the school gym. Max makes a sign with the shape shown below.

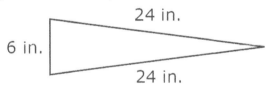

24 in.

6 in.

24 in.

Cal makes a hexagon-shaped sign with 6 equal sides. If Max and Cal have signs with the same perimeter, how long is each side of Cal's sign?

Ⓐ 5 inches   Ⓑ 6 inches   Ⓒ 8 inches   Ⓓ 9 inches

4 A square has side lengths in whole units. Which of these could be the perimeter of the square? Select all the possible answers.

☐ 14 inches   ☐ 16 inches   ☐ 18 inches

☐ 24 inches   ☐ 26 inches   ☐ 27 inches

☐ 35 inches   ☐ 36 inches   ☐ 39 inches

☐ 53 inches   ☐ 75 inches   ☐ 80 inches

5   Carly has two gift boxes. Each gift box has 8 sides of equal length. She wants to decorate them by placing ribbon around all the sides of each box, as shown below.

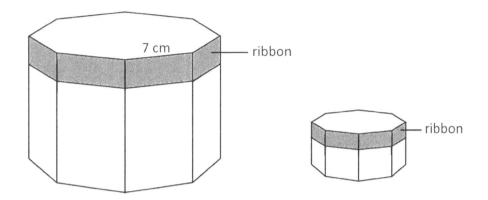

The large box has side lengths of 7 centimeters. How much ribbon will she need to go around the large box exactly once?

Show your work.

Answer _____ cm

She uses 24 centimeters of ribbon to go around the small box exactly once. What is the length of each side of the small box?

Show your work.

Answer _____ cm

A roll of ribbon is 100 centimeters long. How many complete small boxes could she decorate with 1 roll of ribbon?

Show your work.

Answer _____ small boxes

6   Clarissa made four name tags with the shapes shown below.

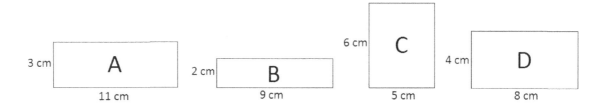

Clarissa wants to place ribbon around the edge of each name tag. The ribbon must go around the edge of each name tag without crossing over. Clarissa has 24 centimeters of ribbon. Answer the questions below by writing the letter or letters of the correct name tags.

For which name tag will she have exactly the right amount of ribbon? _____

Which two name tags will use the same amount of ribbon? _____ and _____

Which name tag does she not have enough ribbon for? _____

7   Gemma starts each soccer practice by running 3 laps around the edges of the soccer field. The diagram below shows the dimensions of the soccer field.

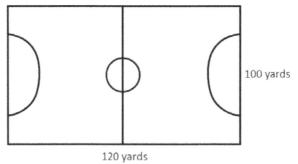

How far does Gemma run to complete the 3 laps?

Show your work.

Answer _____ yards

8   Jay is making masks for a play. He cut the mask below out of cardboard.

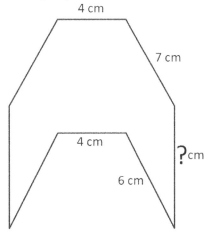

The mask has a perimeter of 50 cm. What is the length of the missing side? Show your work or explain how you found your answer.

Answer _____ cm

9   The four shapes shown below each have equal sides.

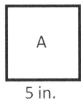   

Mike states that shapes B and D have equal side lengths and so have equal perimeters. Explain why this is incorrect.

_____

_____

_____

Which two shapes do have equal perimeters? _____ and _____

Quiz 40: Relating Area and Perimeter

1   What are the dimensions of a rectangle with an area of 28 square feet and a perimeter of 22 feet?

      Ⓐ 3 by 8 feet   Ⓑ 2 by 14 feet   Ⓒ 7 by 4 feet   Ⓓ 5 by 6 feet

2   The rectangles below all have equal areas. Place the rectangles in order from smallest perimeter to greatest perimeter. Write 1, 2, 3, and 4 on the lines to show the order.

     _____ 2 by 24 cm   _____ 4 by 12 cm   _____ 8 by 6 cm   _____ 16 by 3 cm

3   Jack and Nelson both use 1-inch squares to make a rectangle. They both use 12 squares. Select the statement below that must be true.

    ☐ The rectangles have the same area.

    ☐ The rectangles have the same widths.

    ☐ The rectangles have the same lengths.

    ☐ The rectangles have the same perimeters.

4   Use the shaded shapes numbered 1 through 4 to answer the questions.

        1   2   3   4

Which shapes have the same area but different perimeters? ___ and ___

Which two pairs of shapes have the same perimeter but different areas?

___ and ___, ___ and ___

Which shape has the greatest area? ___

5   Vincent has 20 feet of timber. He wants to use all the timber to make a rectangular frame. Complete the table with the width needed to use all the timber for the given length. Then find the perimeter and area for each set of dimensions. The first one has been completed for you.

Length (ft)	9	8	7	6	5
Width (ft)	1				
Perimeter (ft)	20				
Area (sq. ft)	9				

6   Lexi drew the two figures below.

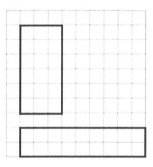

Lexi made the three statements below about the figures. Write "T" or "F" to show whether each statement is true or false.

_____ The two rectangles are both made up of 18 squares.

_____ The two rectangles have the same area.

_____ The two rectangles have the same perimeter.

Complete the sentences to describe the mistake that Lexi made.

Lexi said that _____.

This is incorrect because _____

_____

7   Matthew used logs with a length of 1 meter to put a border around a

garden. Matthew used 20 logs to make the garden shown below.

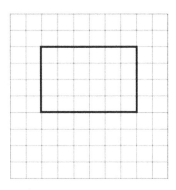

What is the area of Matthew's garden? _____ square meters

Damien made a rectangular garden with the same area, but used 22 logs.
Draw the shape of Damien's garden on the grid.

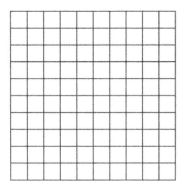

Jonas used 20 logs, but made a rectangular garden with an area of 21 square
meters. Draw the shape of Jonas's garden on the grid below.

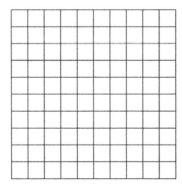

8   Ryan makes a banner that is 6 feet wide and 6 feet high.

What is the area of the banner? _____ square feet

Curtis makes a rectangular banner that has the same area, but a different perimeter. Use the grid to show two possible shapes of Curtis's banner.

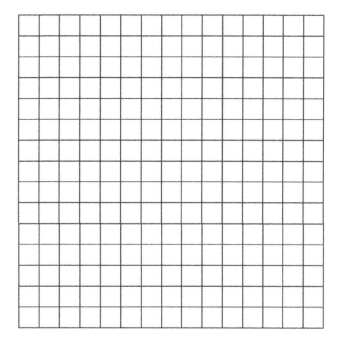

Write three equations to show that the three banners have the same area.

Equation 1:

Equation 2:

Equation 3:

Quizzes 41 to 46

Data

Directions

Read each question carefully. For each multiple-choice question, fill in the circle for the correct answer. For other types of questions, follow the directions given in the question.

You may use a ruler to help you answer questions. You should answer the questions without using a calculator.

COMMON CORE SKILLS LIST
For Parents, Teachers, and Tutors

Quizzes 41 through 46 cover these skills from the Common Core State Standards.

Data

Represent and interpret data.

3. Draw a scaled picture graph and a scaled bar graph to represent a data set with several categories. Solve one- and two-step "how many more" and "how many less" problems using information presented in scaled bar graphs.

4. Generate measurement data by measuring lengths using rulers marked with halves and fourths of an inch. Show the data by making a line plot, where the horizontal scale is marked off in appropriate units—whole numbers, halves, or quarters.

Quiz 41: Drawing Scaled Picture Graphs

1   The table below shows how many points Evan scored in the first eight games of the basketball season.

Evan's Points

Game	Points Scored
1	22
2	26
3	14
4	18
5	20
6	24
7	12
8	10

Complete the picture graph below to represent the data.

Evan's Points

Game	Points Scored
1	OOOOOOOOOOO
2	
3	
4	
5	
6	
7	
8	

Each O = 2 points

2   The table below shows how much money students raised on a fun run.

Money Raised on a Fun Run

Name	Amount Raised ($)
Terry	45
Arnold	25
Cato	50
Grant	20
Jorge	35
Payton	55
Pablo	40
Willis	15

Complete the picture graph below to represent the data.

Money Raised on a Fun Run

Name	Amount Raised ($)
Terry	
Arnold	
Cato	
Grant	
Jorge	
Payton	
Pablo	
Willis	

Each $ = $5

3   The table below shows the number of questions that seven students got correct on a science quiz.

Science Quiz Results

Name	Number of Correct Questions
Isha	14
Jess	18
Kassie	12
Lexis	8
Penny	20
Tessa	16
Renata	24

Choose a suitable scale for the picture graph below. Then complete the picture graph to represent the data.

Science Quiz Results

Each ✓ = _____ correct questions

Name	Number of Correct Questions
Isha	
Jess	
Kassie	
Lexis	
Penny	
Tessa	
Renata	

4   The table below shows how many pieces of pizza a store sold on each day of the week.

Pizza Sales

Day	Number of Pieces
Monday	80
Tuesday	110
Wednesday	90
Thursday	60
Friday	70
Saturday	130
Sunday	150

Choose a suitable scale for the picture graph below. Then complete the picture graph to represent the data.

Each ▷ = _____ pieces of pizza

Pizza Sales

Day	Number of Pieces
Monday	
Tuesday	
Wednesday	
Thursday	
Friday	
Saturday	
Sunday	

Quiz 42: Using Scaled Picture Graphs to Solve Problems

1   The picture graph shows how many emails Pam received each week day.

Pam's Emails

Day	Number of Emails
Monday	✉✉✉
Tuesday	✉✉
Wednesday	✉✉✉✉
Thursday	✉✉✉✉✉✉
Friday	✉✉✉✉✉✉✉✉

Each ✉ means 2 emails.

How many emails did Pam receive on Monday?

_____ emails

How many more emails did Pam receive on Wednesday than on Tuesday?

_____ emails

On which day did Pam receive 6 fewer emails than Thursday?

_____

On which two days did Pam receive a total of 10 emails?

_____ and _____

On which two days did Pam receive the same total number of emails as she received on Friday?

_____ and _____

How many emails were received in all?

_____ emails

2   The picture graph below shows how long Tammy spent at the computer each week day.

Tammy's Computer Time

Day	Computer Time
Monday	 💻💻💻💻
Tuesday	 💻💻💻💻💻💻
Wednesday	 💻💻💻💻💻
Thursday	 💻💻💻
Friday	 💻💻💻💻💻💻💻

Each 💻 means 10 minutes.

How long did Tammy spend at the computer on Monday?

_____ minutes

On which day did Tammy spend 1 hour at the computer?

_____

How much longer did Tammy spend at the computer on Friday than on Thursday?

_____ minutes

How long did Tammy spend at the computer on Monday and Tuesday?

_____ minutes

On which two days did Tammy spend the same time at the computer as Monday and Tuesday combined?

_____ and _____

How long did Tammy spend at the computer in all?

_____ minutes

3   The picture graph shows how many votes seven students received in an election for class president.

Class President Election

Student	Number of Votes
Selena	☺☺☺☺☺☺☺☺
Riley	☺☺☺☺☺
Anton	☺☺☺☺
Tyra	☺☺☺☺☺☺☺☺☺☺☺
Gavin	☺☺☺☺☺
Jett	☺☺☺
Kimi	☺☺☺☺☺☺☺

Each ☺ means 5 votes.

Complete the equation to show how many votes Selena and Riley received in all. Then write the answer.

_____ + _____ = _____   **Answer** _____ votes

Complete the equation to show how many fewer votes Anton received than Tyra. Then write the answer.

_____ - _____ = _____   **Answer** _____ votes

Complete the equation to show how many votes Gavin and Jett received in all. Then write the answer.

_____ + _____ = _____   **Answer** _____ votes

Complete the equation to show how many more votes Kimi received than Jett. Then write the answer.

_____ - _____ = _____   **Answer** _____ votes

4   Kirsten collects pennies. The picture graph below shows how many pennies she added to the collection each month of the year.

Kirsten's Penny Collection

Month	Number of Pennies Added
January	●●●●●◖
February	●●●●◖
March	◖●●●
April	●●●●●●◖
May	●●●●●
June	●●●◖

Each ● means 10 pennies.

Write an equation to show how many more pennies Kirsten collected in January than in February. Then write the answer.

Answer _____ pennies

Write an equation to show how many fewer pennies Kirsten collected in June than in May. Then write the answer.

Answer _____ pennies

Write an equation to show how many pennies Kirsten collected in March and April. Then write the answer.

Answer _____ pennies

Quiz 43: Drawing Scaled Bar Graphs

1   The table below shows the score students received on a spelling quiz.

Spelling Quiz Scores

Name	Score
Ricky	18
Lucy	14
Chan	10
Jed	16
Corey	10
Bevan	12

Complete the bar graph below to represent the data.

Spelling Quiz Scores

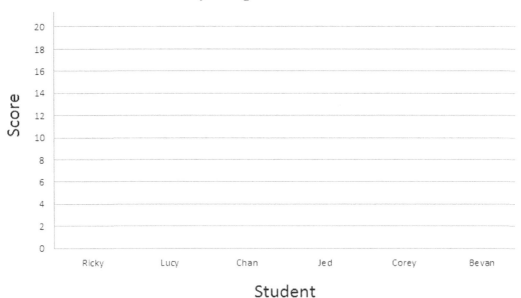

2   The table shows the time Margo spent studying math each week day.

Margo's Math Study Time

Day	Number of Minutes
Monday	60
Tuesday	45
Wednesday	45
Thursday	30
Friday	15

Complete the bar graph below to represent the data. Be sure to include a scale.

Margo's Math Study Time

Number of Minutes

Monday   Tuesday   Wednesday   Thursday   Friday

3   A school has six sporting clubs. The table below shows the number of members each club has.

Sporting Clubs

Club	Number of Members
Baseball	45
Basketball	60
Volleyball	35
Lacrosse	25
Soccer	30
Hockey	40

Complete the bar graph below to represent the data. Be sure to include a scale.

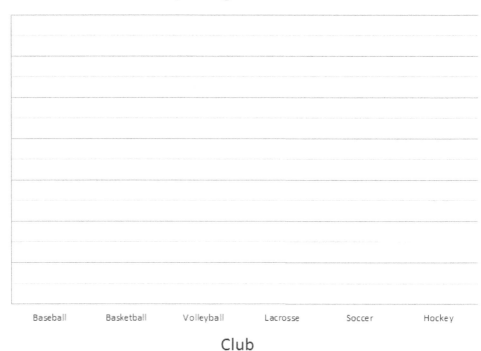

Sporting Clubs

4   A football club had a vote to choose the color of a new mascot. The votes are shown below.

Votes for a New Mascot

Color	Number of Votes
Red	16
Green	18
Blue	14
Yellow	12
Pink	6
Purple	10

Complete the bar graph below to represent the data. Be sure to include a scale and labels on both axes.

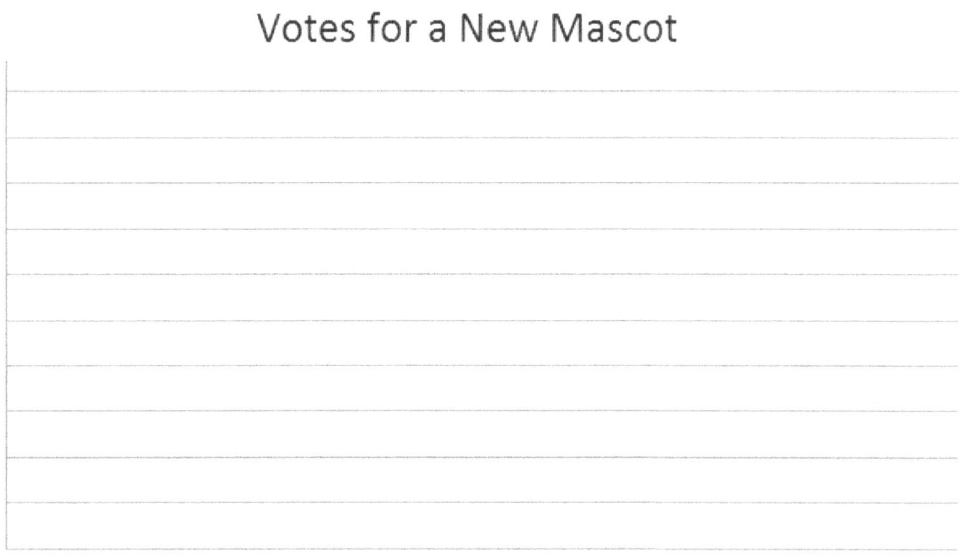

Votes for a New Mascot

Quiz 44: Using Scaled Bar Graphs to Solve Problems

1   Mr. Morgan owns a diner. The graph below shows how many pieces of pie of each type he sold one week. Use the graph to answer the questions.

Pieces of Pie Sold

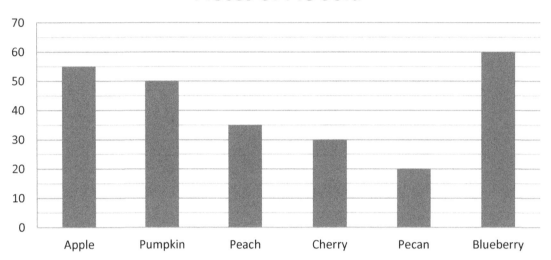

How many more pieces of pumpkin pie were sold than pecan pie? _____

Which type of pie sold 15 more pieces than peach pie? _____

Which type of pie sold 20 fewer pieces than pumpkin pie? _____

Which two types sold a total of 50 pieces? _____ and _____

How many pieces of pecan and blueberry pie were sold in all? _____

Which type of pie sold 3 times as many pieces as pecan pie? _____

Which two types of pie sold the same amount in total as apple pie?

_____ and _____

A piece of cherry pie sells for $3. How much was made from sales of cherry pie? _____

2   The graph below shows how many books seven students read in a month. Use the graph to answer the questions.

Number of Books Read

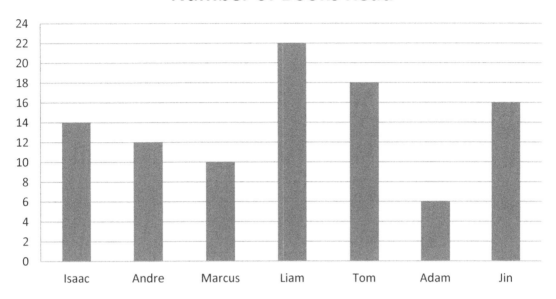

How many more books did Tom read than Marcus? _____

Who read 10 more books than Adam? _____

Which two students read a total of 20 books? _____ and _____

How many books did Isaac and Tom read in all? _____

Who read twice as many books as Adam? _____

How many fewer books did Andre read than Jin? _____

What is the difference between the most and the least books read? _____

List two pairs of students that read a total of 30 books.

1. _____ and _____   2. _____ and _____

3   The graph shows how long Cara spent practicing the piano each day.

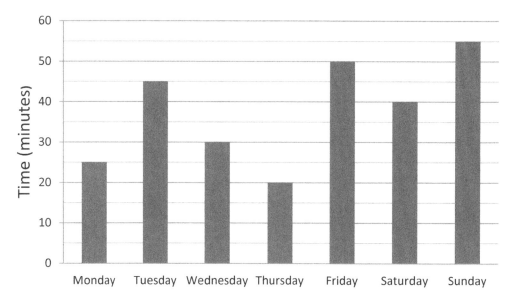

Complete the equation to show how long Cara practiced for on Saturday and Sunday. Then write the answer.

_____ + _____ = _____   **Answer** _____ minutes

Complete the equation to show how much longer Cara practiced for on Tuesday than on Monday. Then write the answer.

_____ - _____ = _____   **Answer** _____ minutes

Complete the equation to show how much longer Cara practiced for on Friday than on Thursday. Then write the answer.

_____ - _____ = _____   **Answer** _____ minutes

Complete the equation to show how long Cara practiced for on Monday, Tuesday, and Wednesday. Then write the answer.

_____ + _____ + _____ = _____   **Answer** _____ minutes

4   Jamie recorded the colors of the cars in a parking lot. The graph below shows the results.

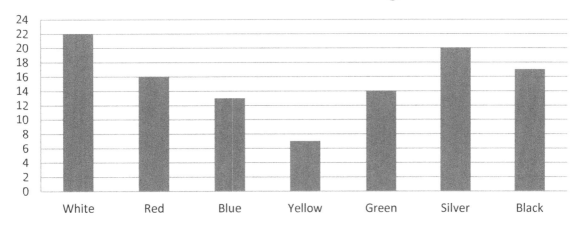

Write an equation to show how many more green cars there were than yellow cars. Then write the answer.

Answer _____ cars

Write an equation to show how many white, black, and silver cars there were in all. Then write the answer.

Answer _____ cars

Jamie says there were more white cars than blue and yellow combined. Is Jamie correct? Explain your answer.

_____

_____

_____

5   The graph shows how many points players scored in a basketball match.

Points Scored in a Basketball Match

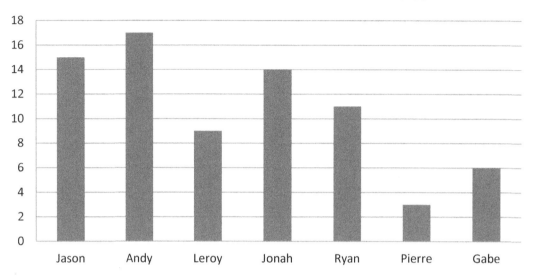

Circle True or False for each statement. Then complete the sentence explaining why the statement is true or false.

Gabe scored twice as many points as Pierre.   True   False

Pierre scored _____ points, and Gabe scored _____ points.

Jonah scored exactly 3 more points than Leroy.   True   False

Jonah scored _____ points, and Leroy scored _____ points.
Jonah scored _____ more points than Leroy.

Jason scored 2 fewer points than Andy.   True   False

Jason scored _____ points, and Andy scored _____ points.

Ryan and Pierre scored a total of 12 points.   True   False

Ryan scored _____ points, and Pierre scored _____ points.
Ryan and Pierre scored a total of _____ points.

6   Amy makes bookmarks to sell at the markets. The graph shows how many bookmarks of each color she sold in May.

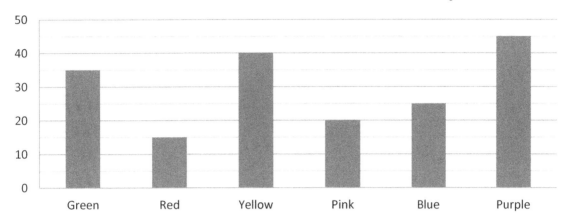

How many more yellow bookmarks than pink bookmarks did she sell?

Show your work.

Answer _____ bookmarks

How many fewer pink bookmarks did she sell than purple bookmarks?

Show your work.

Answer _____ bookmarks

How many bookmarks did she sell in all?

Show your work.

Answer _____ bookmarks

Quiz 45: Measuring Length

1 What is the length of the safety pin to the nearest half inch?

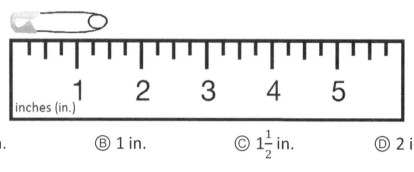

Ⓐ $\frac{1}{2}$ in. Ⓑ 1 in. Ⓒ $1\frac{1}{2}$ in. Ⓓ 2 in.

2 What is the length of the pencil to the nearest quarter inch?

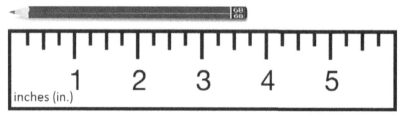

Ⓐ $3\frac{1}{4}$ in. Ⓑ $3\frac{1}{2}$ in. Ⓒ $3\frac{3}{4}$ in. Ⓓ 4 in.

3 What is the length of the fork to the nearest whole inch?

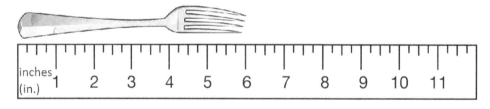

Answer _____ inches

4 What is the length of the bolt to the nearest quarter inch?

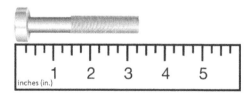

Answer _____ inches

5   Graham placed four candles against a ruler, as shown below.

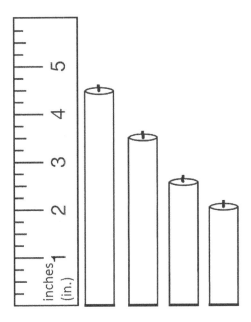

Find the heights of the four candles to the nearest half inch. Record the heights from tallest to shortest.

Tallest   **Shortest**

_____ inches   _____ inches   _____ inches   _____ inches

6   Harriet measured the length of two pieces of ribbon to the nearest quarter inch, as shown below.

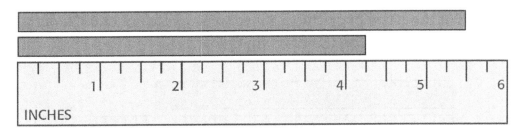

What is the length of the shorter piece of ribbon? _____ inches

What is the length of the longer piece of ribbon? _____ inches

How much longer is one piece of ribbon than the other? _____ inches

7   The brick shown below has a length of $1\frac{1}{2}$ inches. Zane made a wall that is 7 bricks long.

Zane made the diagram below to show the length of 1 brick. Draw rectangles along the ruler below to show the total length of the wall.

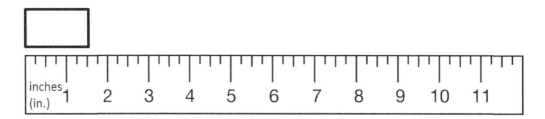

What is the total length of the wall? _____ inches

8   Inga had the piece of cardboard shown below.

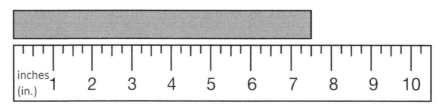

What is the length of the cardboard to the nearest half inch? _____ inches

Inga cut the piece of cardboard into three pieces of equal length. Show the three equal pieces on the diagram below.

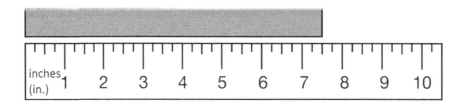

What is the length of each piece? _____ inches

9   The lengths of six crayons are shown below. Write the length of each crayon to the nearest quarter inch.

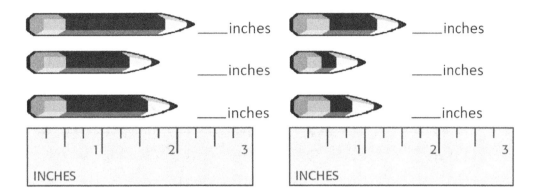

____inches   ____inches

____inches   ____inches

____inches   ____inches

What is the difference in length between the longest and the shortest crayon? Show your work or explain how you found your answer.

Answer _____ inches

10   Chang's bookmark has the length shown below. Margo's bookmark is $\frac{3}{4}$ inches shorter than Chang's. Pierre's bookmark is $\frac{1}{2}$ an inch longer than Chang's. Draw Margo's and Pierre's bookmarks on the diagram below.

Margo

Pierre

Chang

What is the length of the three bookmarks?

Chang _____ inches   **Margo** _____ inches   **Pierre** _____ inches

Quiz 46: Representing Lengths on Line Plots

1   Josie made the line plot below to record the lengths of the carrots she picked from her garden.

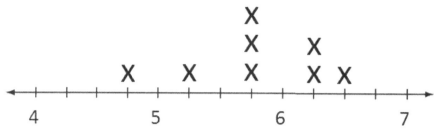

Length of Carrots (inches)

What was the most common carrot length?

Ⓐ $4\frac{3}{4}$ inches   Ⓑ $5\frac{3}{4}$ inches   Ⓒ $6\frac{1}{4}$ inches   Ⓓ $6\frac{1}{2}$ inches

2   The list shows the length of each fish that was caught on a fishing trip.

Length of Fish Caught (inches)

$$7, 7\frac{1}{2}, 6\frac{1}{2}, 6, 7, 8\frac{1}{2}, 8, 6, 7\frac{1}{2}, 8, 8, 6\frac{1}{2}, 6\frac{1}{2}, 8\frac{1}{2}, 7, 6, 6\frac{1}{2}, 8, 7\frac{1}{2}$$

Randall made the line plot below to represent the data, and completed the plot for 6 inches. Finish the line plot by plotting the rest of the data.

```
X
X
X
_____
6        6 1/2       7        7 1/2       8        8 1/2
```

Length of Fish Caught (inches)

3   The table shows the lengths of nine leaves.

Length of Leaves (inches)

Leaf 1	$4\frac{1}{2}$
Leaf 2	$5\frac{1}{2}$
Leaf 3	$4\frac{1}{4}$
Leaf 4	$4\frac{3}{4}$
Leaf 5	$4\frac{1}{2}$
Leaf 6	$4\frac{3}{4}$
Leaf 7	$4\frac{3}{4}$
Leaf 8	5
Leaf 9	$4\frac{3}{4}$

Use the data in the table to complete the line plot below.

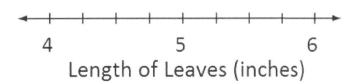

Length of Leaves (inches)

4   Jordan measured the height of tomato plants after 2 weeks of growing. The data she collected is shown below.

Height of Plants (inches)

Plant 1	$2\frac{1}{2}$	Plant 7	$2\frac{3}{4}$
Plant 2	$2\frac{1}{4}$	Plant 8	2
Plant 3	$2\frac{1}{4}$	Plant 9	$1\frac{3}{4}$
Plant 4	$1\frac{3}{4}$	Plant 10	$2\frac{1}{2}$
Plant 5	$2\frac{1}{2}$	Plant 11	$2\frac{1}{4}$
Plant 6	$2\frac{3}{4}$	Plant 12	$1\frac{3}{4}$

Use the data in the table to complete the line plot below.

$1\frac{1}{2}$ $1\frac{3}{4}$ 2 $2\frac{1}{4}$ $2\frac{1}{2}$ $2\frac{3}{4}$ 3

Height of Plants (inches)

How many plants had a height of 2 inches or more? _____ plants

Explain how you used the line plot to find the answer.

_____

_____

5   The lengths of eight pencils are shown below.

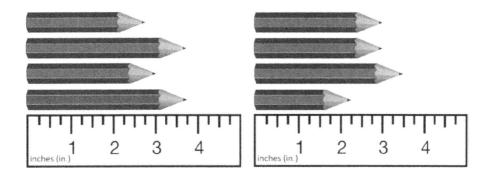

List the length of each pencil to the nearest quarter inch.

Length of Pencils (inches)

Use the data collected to complete the line plot below.

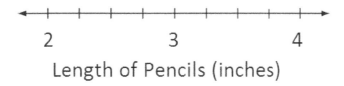

Length of Pencils (inches)

Which pencil length is the most common? _____ inches

Describe how the line plot makes it easier to compare how common each length is.

_____

_____

_____

Quizzes 47 to 52

Geometry

Directions

Read each question carefully. For each multiple-choice question, fill in the circle for the correct answer. For other types of questions, follow the directions given in the question.

You may use a ruler to help you answer questions. You should answer the questions without using a calculator.

COMMON CORE SKILLS LIST
For Parents, Teachers, and Tutors

Quizzes 47 through 52 cover these skills from the Common Core State Standards.

Geometry

Reason with shapes and their attributes.

1. Understand that shapes in different categories (e.g., rhombuses, rectangles, and others) may share attributes (e.g., having four sides), and that the shared attributes can define a larger category (e.g., quadrilaterals). Recognize rhombuses, rectangles, and squares as examples of quadrilaterals, and draw examples of quadrilaterals that do not belong to any of these subcategories.

2. Partition shapes into parts with equal areas. Express the area of each part as a unit fraction of the whole. *For example, partition a shape into 4 parts with equal area, and describe the area of each part as 1/4 of the area of the shape.*

Quiz 47: Understanding the Properties of Shapes

1   A rectangle and a trapezoid are shown below.

Which of the following do these shapes always have in common?

Ⓐ number of sides   Ⓑ right angles

Ⓒ pairs of equal sides   Ⓓ side lengths

2   A rhombus is shown below.

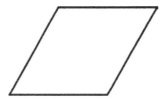

Which sentence best explains why a rhombus is a quadrilateral?

Ⓐ It has equal sides.   Ⓑ It has parallel sides.

Ⓒ It has four sides.   Ⓓ It has no right angles.

3   What do all the shapes shown below have in common? Select all the correct answers.

☐ total number of sides   ☐ right angles

☐ length of the sides   ☐ four equal angles

☐ height of the sides   ☐ four equal sides

4   The flag of the Bahamas is shown below.

What type of quadrilateral makes up part of the flag? _____

Based on the number of sides, which other two shapes make up the flag?

_____ and _____

5   Sort the shapes shown below into pentagons and hexagons. Write the letters in the table to sort the shapes.

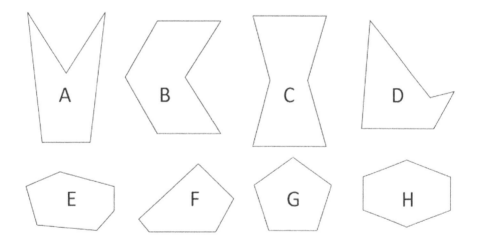

Pentagons	Hexagons

Complete the sentences to describe the pentagons and hexagons.

The pentagons all have ____ sides.

The hexagons all have ____ sides.

6 Felix places 5 straws of equal length end to end to make a closed shape.

Sketch the shape that Felix made in the space below.

How many sides does the shape have? _____

How many angles does the shape have? _____

What is the name of the shape? _____

7 Annabelle states that the shapes below are all parallelograms because they all have a pair of parallel sides.

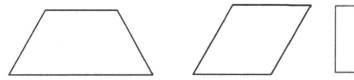

Is Annabelle correct? Explain why or why not.

_____

_____

_____

_____

8   Which shapes described can have at least one right angle? Select all the correct answers.

☐ square with a side length of 4 units

☐ rhombus with 2 pairs of equal angles

☐ rectangle with a height twice its width

☐ trapezoid with parallel sides of 2 units and 5 units

Draw an example of each shape you selected with at least one right angle.

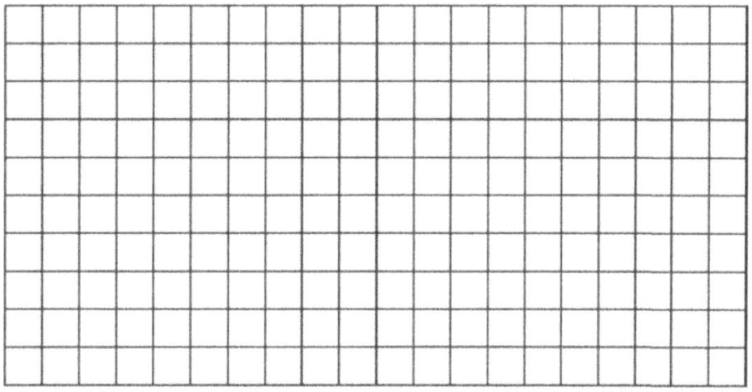

9   Jasmine drew the three shapes shown below.

What do the three shapes have in common?

_____

_____

What makes the first two shapes different from the last shape?

_____

_____

Quiz 48: Comparing Shapes

1   Which shape has more sides than a pentagon?

Ⓐ triangle   Ⓑ rectangle   Ⓒ octagon   Ⓓ trapezoid

2   Order the shapes below from least to most sides. Write the numbers 1, 2, 3, and 4 on the lines to show the order.

_____ hexagon   _____ octagon   _____ pentagon   _____ square

3   Dorian and Marco both drew octagons. Which statement must be true of the figures Dorian and Marco drew?

Ⓐ They must be exactly the same.

Ⓑ They must have the same number of angles.

Ⓒ They must have the same side lengths.

Ⓓ They must have the same angle measures.

4   Tavena sketched the four triangles shown below. Answer the questions below by writing the correct letter on each line.

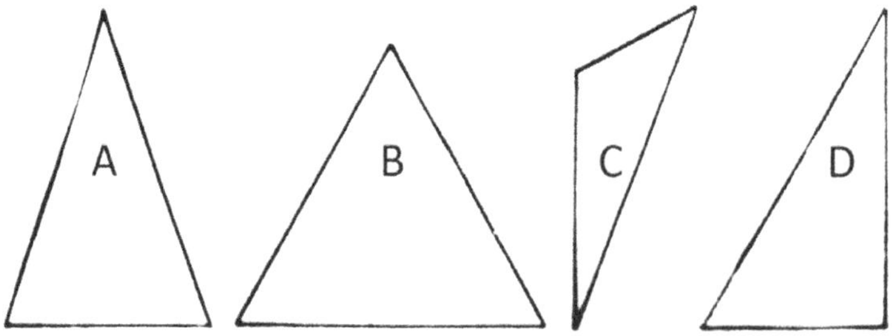

Which triangle has a right angle? _____

Which triangle has exactly two equal angles? _____

Which triangle has all sides of equal length? _____

Which two triangles have no sides of equal length? _____ and _____

5   Complete the table below by describing each feature of a square and a rectangle.

Feature	Square	Rectangle
Number of Sides		
Number of Angles		
Right Angles		
Parallel Sides		
Equal Sides		

Based on the table, which feature can be used to tell a square and a rectangle apart?

_____

_____

6   Describe three ways a square is similar to a rhombus.

1. _____

2. _____

3. _____

Describe two ways a square is different from a rhombus.

1. _____

2. _____

7   Two shapes are shown below.

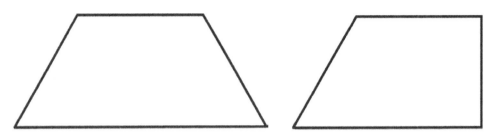

What do the two shapes have in common?

_____

_____

What makes the second shape different from the first?

_____

_____

8   For each group of shapes below, draw a fourth shape that fits in the same category in the empty circle.

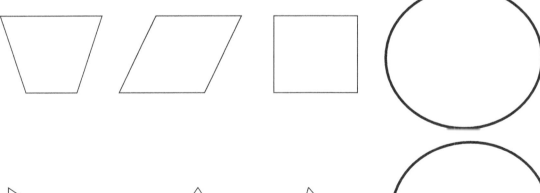

9   On each grid below, draw a polygon with the description given.

Draw a polygon with the same number of sides as a square, but no sides of equal length.	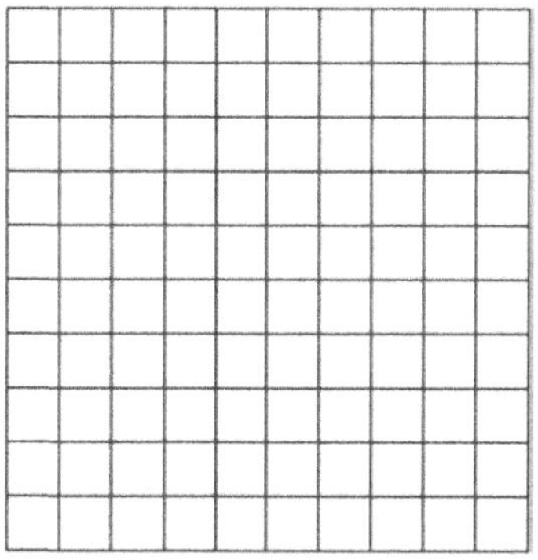
Draw a polygon with 1 less side than an octagon.	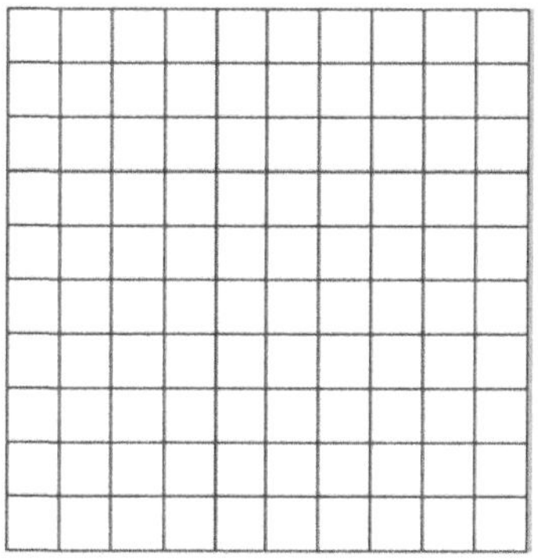
Draw a polygon with twice as many sides as a triangle.	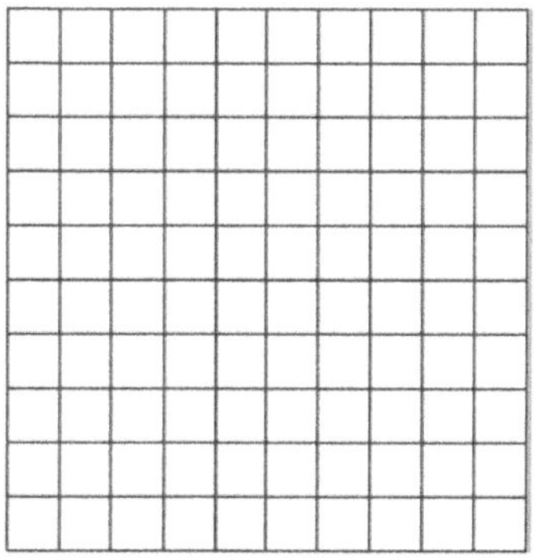
Draw a polygon with the same number of sides as the shape shown below, but no sides of equal length. 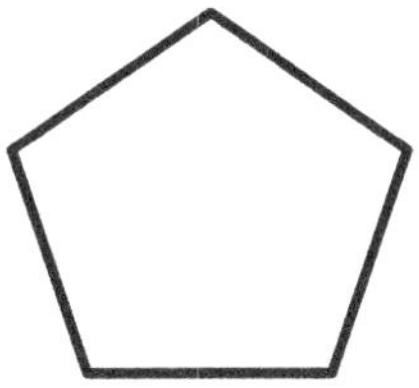	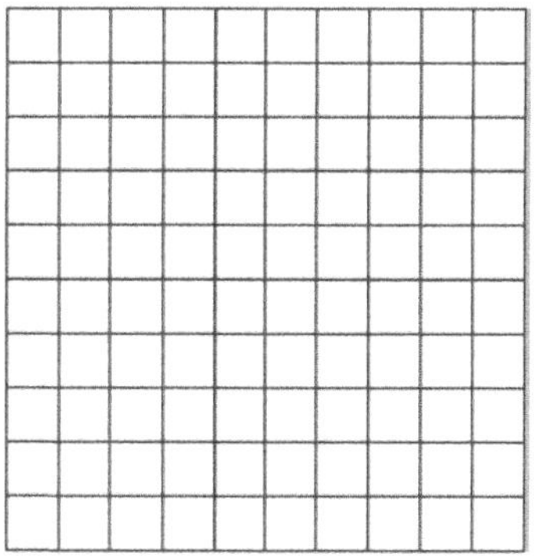

Quiz 49: Classifying Shapes

1   Which term describes the three shapes shown below?

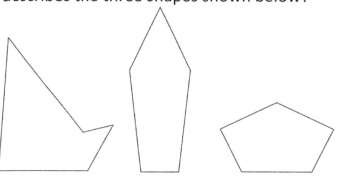

Ⓐ octagon   Ⓑ pentagon   Ⓒ hexagon   Ⓓ quadrilateral

2   What is the shape of the outside of the nut shown below?

Ⓐ hexagon   Ⓑ octagon   Ⓒ pentagon   Ⓓ square

3   Which statement is true about rhombuses and rectangles?

Ⓐ They always have 4 equal sides.

Ⓑ They always have 4 right angles.

Ⓒ They always have 4 equal angles.

Ⓓ They always have 4 sides.

4   Two shapes both have four equal sides. Which of these could the two shapes be?

Ⓐ square and rectangle

Ⓑ square and rhombus

Ⓒ rhombus and rectangle

Ⓓ square and trapezoid

5   A quadrilateral has 4 equal angles. Which question should be asked to determine if the shape is a rectangle or a square?

Ⓐ What is the measure of each angle?

Ⓑ Is the shape a parallelogram?

Ⓒ Are all the sides of the shape equal?

Ⓓ Does the shape have right angles?

6   Select all the shapes listed below that are parallelograms.

☐ square   ☐ trapezoid   ☐ rectangle

☐ rhombus   ☐ triangle   ☐ pentagon

7   Circle all the figures below that are octagons.

 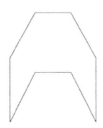 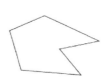 

On the lines below, describe what characteristic all the octagons have in common.

_____

_____

8   Which two polygons make up the sides of each figure shown below? Write your answers on the lines next to each shape.

_____ and _____

_____ and _____

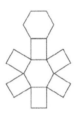

_____ and _____

_____ and _____

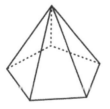

_____ and _____

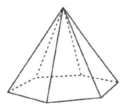

_____ and _____

9   Look at the shapes below.

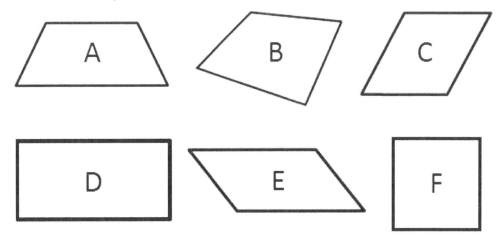

Which shape is a rhombus but not a square? _____

Describe three features that tell that the shape is a rhombus.

1. _____

2. _____

3. _____

Which shape is a trapezoid? _____

Describe two features that tell that the shape is a trapezoid.

1. _____

2. _____

Which shape is a square? _____

Describe two features that tell that the shape is a square.

1. _____

2. _____

Quiz 50: Identifying and Drawing Quadrilaterals

1   Which shape below is a quadrilateral?

  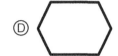

2   Select all the shapes below that are trapezoids.

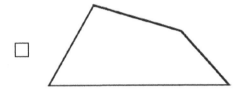

3   Amber drew a quadrilateral by drawing four lines of equal length. Draw the two quadrilaterals she could have drawn below and name each one.

Name _____   **Name** _____

4   Kane placed shapes together to make images of different items. The diagrams below show the images he made. For each image, complete the sentences to describe the number of each shape used.

	He used 1 _____. He used 1 _____. He used 5 _____.
	He used 1 _____. He used 2 _____. He used 3 _____.
	He used 1 _____. He used 1 _____. He used 1 _____. He used 5 _____.
	He used 1 _____. He used 2 _____. He used 3 _____.

5   Circle all the shapes below that are quadrilaterals.

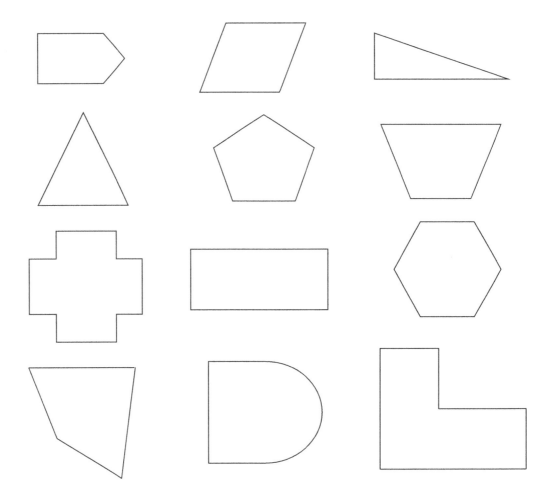

Which two quadrilaterals are also parallelograms? Name the shapes.

_____ and _____

In the space below, draw another quadrilateral that is a parallelogram and name the shape.

Name _____

6   On each grid below, draw a quadrilateral with the description given and name the shape.

Draw a parallelogram with two sides of 8 units each, and two sides of 4 units each.

Name _____

Draw a shape with one right angle and exactly two parallel sides.

Name _____

Draw a quadrilateral with four equal sides, but no right angles.

Name _____

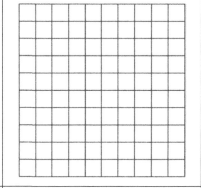

Draw a quadrilateral with four sides of 5 units each, and four equal angles.

Name _____

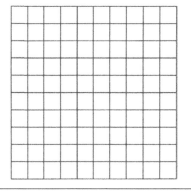

Quiz 51: Dividing Shapes into Equal Parts

1   What fraction of the shape below is shaded?

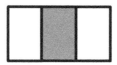

Ⓐ $\frac{1}{2}$ Ⓑ $\frac{1}{3}$ Ⓒ $\frac{1}{4}$ Ⓓ $\frac{1}{6}$

2   Harriet made a bookmark by drawing stripes on a piece of cardboard, as shown below.

What fraction of the cardboard does each stripe cover?

Ⓐ $\frac{1}{2}$ Ⓑ $\frac{1}{4}$ Ⓒ $\frac{1}{6}$ Ⓓ $\frac{1}{8}$

3   Which of these shows one way to divide a hexagon into two parts with equal areas?

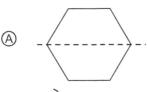

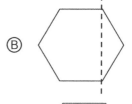

4   Which of these shapes can be divided into two equal triangles? Select all the correct answers.

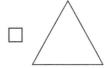      

5   Divide each shape below into two triangles of equal areas.

6   Bailey divided circles into two equal parts, as shown below. Draw additional lines to divide the other circles into the number of parts given.

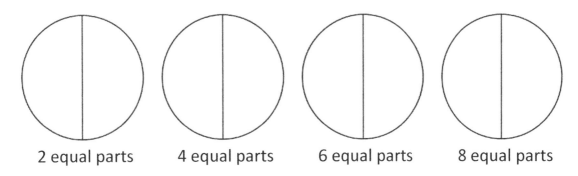

2 equal parts   4 equal parts   6 equal parts   8 equal parts

7   Divide each rectangle shown below into the number of parts given.

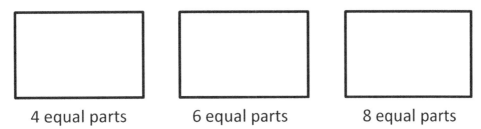

4 equal parts   6 equal parts   8 equal parts

8   For each shape shown below, divide it into 3 parts with equal areas.

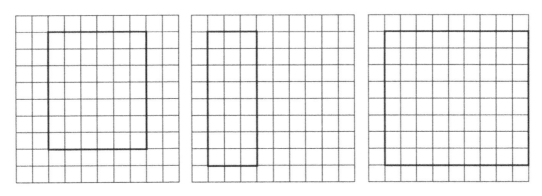

Quiz 52: Using Shapes to Understand Fractions

1   Students were asked to divide a triangle into equal halves. The diagram below shows how four students divided the shape.

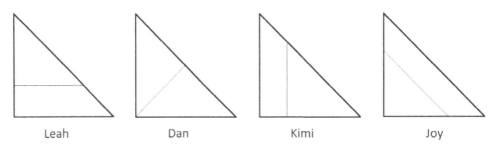

Which student divided the triangle correctly?

Ⓐ Leah   Ⓑ Dan   Ⓒ Kimi   Ⓓ Joy

2   Which circle below is divided into parts of $\frac{1}{5}$ each?

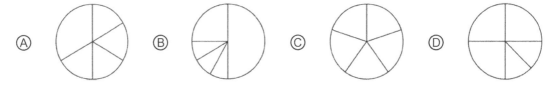

3   Which figure has $\frac{1}{4}$ shaded?

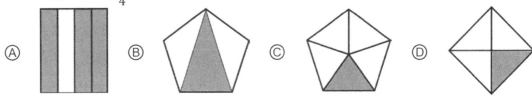

4   A pie is divided into pieces of $\frac{1}{6}$ of a pie each.

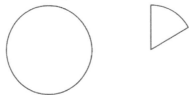

How many pieces make up a whole pie? _____ pieces

5   Divide each shape shown below into parts of equal area and shade the fraction given.

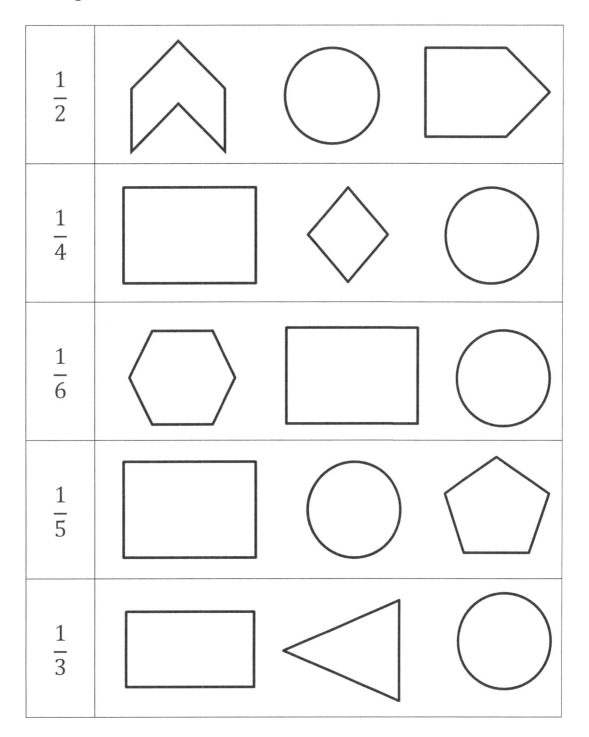

6 Students were asked to shade $\frac{1}{4}$ of a square. Four answers are below.

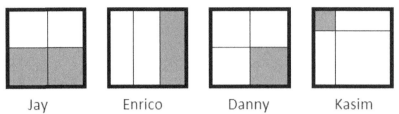

    Jay   Enrico   Danny   Kasim

Which student shaded the square correctly? _____

Complete the sentences to describe the mistake three students made.

Jay shaded ___ parts instead of ___.

Enrico divided the square into ___ parts instead of ___.

_____ did not divide the square into equal parts.

7 Students were asked to shade $\frac{1}{4}$ of a rectangle. Four answers are below.

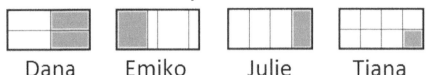

   Dana   Emiko   Julie   Tiana

Which student shaded the rectangle correctly? _____

Write a sentence to describe the mistake the other three students made.

1. _____

_____

2. _____

_____

3. _____

_____

8   Which fraction is represented by each row of the fraction strip?

Answer _____

9   Kate divided the circle below into parts and stated that the circle is divided into thirds. Divide the second circle below into thirds correctly.

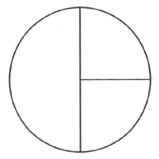   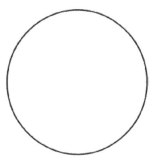

Explain why Kate's circle is not divided into thirds correctly and the circle you divided is.

_____

_____

10   The grid below shows $\frac{1}{4}$ of a shape. Complete the shape to show the complete shape.

ANSWER KEY

Quizzes 1 to 12: Operations and Algebraic Thinking

Quiz 1: Understanding Multiplication

1. C **2.** D **3.** 2nd and 6th **4.** 64 pencils **5.** $6 \times 5 = 30$, $9 \times 3 = 27$, $8 \times 10 = 80$, $6 \times 7 = 42$, $5 \times 8 = 40$
6. Any four of the following: 2, 24; 24, 2; 3, 16; 16, 3; 4, 12; 12, 4; 6, 8; 8, 6.
7. Example: There were 7 boxes of water on a truck. Each box had 24 bottles in it. How many bottles were there?
8. Example: Davis had 3 basketball lessons. Each basketball lesson went for 60 minutes. How long were all the basketball lessons?
9. Example: Joe bought 15 notepads for $3 each. How much did he spend?
10. 2 / 2×6 / 12, 3 / 3×6 / 18, 4 / 4×6 / 24, 5 / 5×6 / 30 **11.** 2 rows of 8, 8 rows of 2, or 4 rows of 4; $2 \times 8 = 16$ or $4 \times 4 = 16$ **12.** $3 \times 6 \times 4 = 72$; 72 stickers

Quiz 2: Understanding Division

1. A **2.** C **3.** 1st and 3rd **4.** $30 \div 6 = 5$, $28 \div 4 = 7$, $72 \div 9 = 8$, $32 \div 4 = 8$ **5.** $40 \div 8 = 5$
6. 4, 5, and 8 circled; $80 \div 4 = 20$, $80 \div 5 = 16$, $80 \div 8 = 10$
7. Example: There are 24 students in a class. They are sorted into 6 teams. How many students are in each team?
8. Example: Morgan has 36 baseball cards. He puts 4 cards on each page of an album. How many pages does he fill?
9. Example: Anna has 50 candies. She divided them between 10 children. How many candies does each child get?
10. 5 lots of 4 apples circled; 4 apples **11.** diagram of 3 sets of 4 quarters; $12 \div 4 = 3$
12. $18 \div 3 = 6$; 6 tomatoes

Quiz 3: Using Multiplication to Solve Problems

1. B **2.** C **3.** 3, 4, 2, 1 **4.** 1st and 4th **5.** 20, 36, 44, 52 circled; 40 pounds **6.** 6, 8; 48 people ($6 \times 8 = 48$); 8 tables ($48 \div 6 = 8$) **7.** Paolo; Trey **8.** 4 / 24 / 12, 6 / 36 / 18, 8 / 48 / 24, 10 / 60 / 30
9. 24 roses **10.** $42 **11.** 15 planks of wood ($5 \times 3 = 15$), 20 feet ($5 \times 4 = 20$) **12.** 4 lettuces (work shows 6 rows of 4 lettuces and 4 left over)

Quiz 4: Using Division to Solve Problems

1. B **2.** D **3.** 1st, 4th, and 5th **4.** 8 pounds **5.** 12 fish tanks **6.** 5 cakes ($80 \div (8 \times 2)$ or $80 \div 2 \div 8$)
7. $4 ($8 \times 3 = 24$, $24 \div 6 = 4$) **8.** $6 ($12 \times 4 = 48$, $48 \div 8 = 6$) **9.** 6, 4, 32, 3 **10.** 24 cups, 7 cartons, 8 cartons, 40 cups **11.** $18 \div 2 = 9$, 18, 2, 9; $18 \div 3 = 6$, 18, 6 **12.** Ivy, 10 tiles ($50 \div 5 = 10$ or $5 \times 10 = 50$); Amelia, 6 tiles ($54 \div 9 = 6$ or $9 \times 6 = 54$); Tori and Dina ($8 \times 8 = 64$, $7 \times 7 = 49$)

Quiz 5: Using Properties of Numbers

1. A **2.** A **3.** 24 ÷ 6 = 4, 24 ÷ 4 = 6; 42 ÷ 7 = 6, 42 ÷ 6 = 7; 27 ÷ 3 = 9, 27 ÷ 9 = 3; 32 ÷ 8 = 4, 32 ÷ 4 = 8; 35 ÷ 5 = 7, 35 ÷ 7 = 5; 72 ÷ 9 = 8, 72 ÷ 8 = 9 **4.** 4 × 9 = 36, 9 × 4 = 36; 4 × 5 = 20, 5 × 4 = 20; 2 × 9 = 18, 9 × 2 = 18; 8 × 6 = 48, 6 × 8 = 48; 6 × 5 = 30, 5 × 6 = 30; 4 × 7 = 28, 7 × 4 = 28
5. 6, 1, 6, 9, 4, 8, 5, 3, 7 **6.** 6 × 8, 48; 8 × 9, 72; 2 × 6, 12; 6 × 4, 24; 9 × 7, 63
7. (4 × 6) + (4 × 2), 32 **8.** 9 × (4 + 5) and (9 × 3) + (9 × 6) **9.** C **10.** (10 × 2) + (4 × 2) = 20 + 8 = 28; (10 × 4) + (8 × 4) = 40 + 32 = 72; (20 × 6) + (5 × 6) = 120 + 30 = 150; (30 × 3) + (6 × 3) = 90 + 18 = 108; (10 × 3) + (5 × 3) = 30 + 15 = 45; (40 × 5) + (3 × 5) = 200 + 15 = 215; (20 × 7) + (8 × 7) = 140 + 56 = 196; (50 × 7) + (2 × 7) = 350 + 14 = 364 **11.** 2 × 5 = 10, then 10 × 6 = 60; 2 × 6 = 12, then 12 × 5 = 60; 5 × 6 = 30, then 30 × 2 = 60 **12.** (2 × 10) + (2 × 6), 32 coins; the coins are divided into two groups of 16 coins each, (2 × 8) + (2 × 8) or (1 × 16) + (1 × 16), 32 coins

Quiz 6: Using Multiplication and Division Equations

1. B **2.** C **3.** 72 ÷ __ = 9, 72 ÷ 9 = __, 9 × __ = 72, __ × 9 = 72 **4.** A **5.** 30 ÷ __ = 10, 3; __ × 6 = 42, 7; __ × 2 = 12, 6; __ ÷ 5 = 7, 35 **6.** 6 × 2, 3 × 4; 8 × 2, 4 × 4; 9 × 2, 3 × 6; 10 × 2, 5 × 4; 12 × 2, 8 × 3, 6 × 4; 15 × 2, 10 × 3, 6 × 5; 20 × 2, 10 × 4, 8 × 5 **7.** 56 ÷ 8 = 7, 7 pages; 7 × 4 = 28, 28 stickers **8.** 72 ÷ 8 = 9, 9 bags; 9 × 4 = 36, $36 **9.** 28 ÷ 4 = 7, 7 tables; 7 × 3 = 21, 21 sunflowers
10. 27 ÷ 3 = 9, 9 groups; 9 × 5 = 45, 45 leaves

Quiz 7: Using Multiplication Facts

1. B **2.** C **3.** A **4.** 42 ÷ __ = 7, 48 ÷ 8 = __, 10 × __ = 60 **5.** 21, 24, 16, 81, 28, 9, 30, 56, 42, 36, 4, 40, 24, 35, 12 **6.** 9, 3, 9, 10, 6, 5, 1, 8, 10, 6, 8, 5 **7.** 7, 2; 9, 3; 8, 4; 7, 5; 6, 8; 9, 7; 8, 8; 9, 6; 5, 5
8. 16, 16 ÷ 2 = 8; 63, 63 ÷ 9 = 7; 20, 20 ÷ 4 = 5; 27, 27 ÷ 3 = 9 **9.** B **10.** 20, 24, 28, 32 should be circled; Only numbers that are multiples of 4 or can be divided evenly by 4 are possible.

Quiz 8: Using Division Facts

1. B **2.** D **3.** A **4.** 21 ÷ __ = 7, 3 ÷ 1 = __, 15 ÷ 5 = __, 10 × __ = 30, __ × 9 = 27 **5.** 6, 8 **6.** 6, 8, 7, 10, 6, 7, 7, 10, 9, 8, 5, 3, 9, 7, 9 **7.** 4, 4, 9, 3, 9, 6, 4, 9, 8 **8.** 21, 30, 30, 16, 45, 4, 40, 48, 81 **9.** 8, 8 × 8 = 64; 9, 9 × 4 = 36; 7, 7 × 2 = 14; 8, 8 × 6 = 48 **10.** 32 ÷ 4 = 8, 70 ÷ 7 = 10, 18 ÷ 3 = 6, 56 ÷ 8 = 7, 27 ÷ 9 = 3 **11.** The student should explain that 8 is not a factor of 30 or that 8 does not divide evenly into 30. The student should give a way of dividing 30 evenly, such as 5 teams of 6 players each or 3 teams of 10 players each.

Quiz 9: Solving Word Problems

1. A **2.** D **3.** C **4.** C **5.** Denzel and Colin; Denzel and Wes; 4 **6.** 240 apples ($3 \times 20 = 60$, $60 \times 4 = 240$) **7.** $83 ($8 \times 6 = 48$, $48 + 35 = 83$) **8.** 42 pieces of pie ($12 \times 8 = 96$, $96 - 54 = 42$) **9.** 4 packs of nails ($6 \times 10 = 60$, $60 \div 15 = 4$) **10.** 7 weeks (The student could find the total amount each week by completing a list or a table, could use equations or show calculations, or could use a written explanation.) **11.** 410 grams (The student could show the work using a list, table, equations, calculations, or a written description.) **12.** 16 days (The student could show the work using a list, table, equations, calculations, or a written description.) **13.** 30 oranges ($12 \div 4 = 3$, $3 \times 10 = 30$); $27 (bananas 2 lots for $3 each, apples 3 lots for $2 each, pears 5 lots for $3 each, $6 + 6 + 15 = 27$); 24 pears ($20 - 8 = 12$, $12 buys 4 lots of 6 pears each, $4 \times 6 = 24$); 20 oranges and 12 pears (20 oranges for $8, 12 pears for $6)

Quiz 10: Representing Word Problems with Equations

1. B **2.** B **3.** B **4.** D **5.** $72 \div n = 8$, $8 \times n = 72$, $72 \div 8 = n$, $n \times 8 = 72$ **6.** 1st and 3rd, 2nd and 4th, 3rd and 1st, 4th and 2nd **7.** __ $\times 5 = 45$, 9; __ $- 12 = 20$, 32; $20 \div$ __ $= 4$, 5; __ $+ 13 = 30$, 17; __ $\div 10 = 5$, 50; __ $- 4 = 24$, 28; __ $\times 7 = 28$, 4 **8.** $6 \times 9 + 2 = c$ **9.** $62 + 48 - 85 = p$, 25 pennies **10.** $60 + 20 + m = 120$, 40 minutes **11.** $(80 - 30) \div 5 = d$, 10 days **12.** $380 - 170 - 140 = m$ or $170 + 140 + m = 380$, 70 miles **13.** $(36 + 28) \div 4 = b$, 16 boxes of tiles **14.** $22 + x = 86$ or $86 - 22 = x$, 64 points; $3 \times x = 120$ or $120 \div 3 = x$, 40 minutes; $12 - 9 = x$ or $9 + x = 12$, 3 free throws; $86 - 9 = x$ or $86 - x = 9$, 77 points

Quiz 11: Using Estimation and Rounding

1. D **2.** A **3.** C **4.** C **5.** B **6.** B **7.** $70 \times 3 = 210$, $80 \times 3 = 240$, between 210 and 240; $20 \times 5 = 100$, $30 \times 5 = 150$, between 100 and 150; $80 \times 6 = 480$, $90 \times 6 = 540$, between 480 and 540 **8.** $1800 - 1200 = 600$, 600 books; $1800 - 1400 = 400$, 400 books; $1400 + 1800 + 1200 = 4400$, 4400 books **9.** $280, $220, $370; $130 ($1000 - 280 - 220 - 370 = 130$ or $1000 - (280 + 220 + 370) = 130$) **10.** 60 miles ($180 \div 3 = 60$) **11.** 150 seats ($500 - 350 = 150$) **12.** 700 visitors ($240 + 260 + 200 = 700$; Sunday (The student may find $4000 \div 20 = 200$ and state that Sunday's figure is closest to 200. The student could also estimate ticket sales for each day and find that Sunday's estimate is $4000.) **13.** He would have saved over $240. $8 \times 30 = 240$. 32 is greater than 30, so 8×32 is greater than 240. **14.** $4 \times 10 = 40$ and 9 is less than 10, so 4×9 is less than 40

Quiz 12: Understanding Patterns

1. B **2.** A **3.** C **4.** D **5.** B **6.** 14, 18, 22, 26, 30, 34, 38 **7.** A **8.** 2, 3; 3, 2; 40, 4; 1, 5; 100, 11; 1, 4 **9.** 24, 27; 26, 30, $n + 4$; 18, 12, $n - 6$; 4, 2, $n \div 2$; 32, 64, $n \times 2$ **10.** Odd A, E, G; Even C, H, J Odd and Even B, D, F, I **11.** 16, 6; 24, 9; 32, 12; 40, 15; 48, 18; The total number of rolls is always a multiple of 8 and 8 is even.; The total cost is a multiple of 3, which can be odd or even. **12.** 42, 48, 54, 60; There are 6 trees in each row, so the total amount must be able to be evenly divided by 6.

Quizzes 13 to 18: Number and Operations in Base Ten

Quiz 13: Understanding and Using Place Value

1. C **2.** C **3.** B **4.** B **5.** 67, 60, 365, 5,364 **6.** D **7.** 8, 9; 6, 5; 4, 2; 9, 7, 5; 7, 0, 3; 5, 4, 0 **8.** 6, 8, 4; 7, 5, 9; 4, 0, 3; 1, 6, 0 **9.** 6, 8, 2; 2, 9, 5; 3, 0, 4; 5, 7, 0 **10.** 998, 133, 999, 743, 135, 655, 158, 659 **11.** 448, 565, 427, 177, 286, 563, 736, 908 **12.** 20, 400, 40, 300, 2, 600, 90, 70, 400, 30, 12, 25, 34, 51, 35 **13.** 367 and 376; the two smallest numbers have the lowest number in the hundreds place **14.** Sal's estimate is closest. Rounding to the nearest ten gives numbers closer to the original than rounding to the nearest hundred. (The student could also complete the rounded calculations and compare the results.)

Quiz 14: Rounding Whole Numbers

1. C **2.** D **3.** 652, 653, 647, 651 **4.** 842, 803, 848, 826, 817 **5.** 770, 800 **6.** 1230, 1200 **7.** 690, 700; 520, 500; 190, 200; 360, 400; 60, 100; 730, 700; 130, 100; 810, 800; 260, 300; 910, 900 **8.** Any number in the following ranges from top to bottom: 425 to 434, 85 to 94, 675 to 684, 125 to 134, 105 to 114, 185 to 194, 685 to 694, 455 to 464, 335 to 344, 705 to 714 **9.** 1, ones; 6, ones; 4, tens; 5, tens **10.** numbers 85 to 94 plotted **11.** 45, 54; 275, 284; 395, 404; 1755, 1764 **12.** 8780, 8800; The number 2 in the ones place is less than 5, and so the number is rounded down to the nearest ten. The number 8 in the tens place is more than 5, so the number is rounded up to the nearest hundred. **13.** 4 and 6; 1, 3, and 7; 64, The highest number that rounds to 60 is 64. Any number 65 or greater would be rounded to 70.; All the scores would be rounded up, so the estimate would be greater. **14.** Jessica did not realize that the number could be less than 700. The numbers 650 through 699 also round to 700.

Quiz 15: Adding Whole Numbers

1. D **2.** B **3.** D **4.** 779, 914, 578, 410, 379, 830, 770, 700, 706, 909, 809, 840, 610, 600, 600, 860 **5.** 52 + 48, 3 + 82 + 15, 62 + 28 + 10 **6.** 244 + 213 **7.** 19, 12; 66, 89; 23, 55; 71, 27 **8.** 79 − 44 = 35, 79 − 35 = 44; 129 − 77 = 52, 129 − 52 = 77; 113 − 24 = 89, 113 − 89 = 24; 293 − 152 = 141, 293 − 141 = 152; 590 − 305 = 285, 590 − 285 = 305; 752 − 641 = 111, 752 − 111 = 641 **9.** 60 + 10 = 70, 3 + 9 = 12, 70 + 12 = 82; 20 + 40 = 60, 7 + 8 = 15, 60 + 15 = 75; 30 + 20 = 50, 1 + 6 = 7, 50 + 7 = 57; 70 + 10 = 80, 5 + 7 = 12, 80 + 12 = 92; 50 + 30 = 80, 8 + 8 = 16, 80 + 16 = 96 **10.** 49 miles (18 + 19 + 12 = 49) **11.** 1007 visitors (586 + 421 = 1007) **12.** 293 stamps (111 + 182 = 293); 404 stamps (293 + 111 = 404) **13.** 138 + 262 = 400, 400 + 85 = 485; The numbers 138 and 262 add to a whole hundred, and it is easier to add 85 to a whole hundred. **14.** 65 + 35 = 100, 100 + 47 = 147; 29 + 71 = 100, 100 + 34 = 134; 88 + 32 = 120, 120 + 67 = 187; 26 + 44 = 70, 70 + 57 = 127

Quiz 16: Subtracting Whole Numbers

1. B **2.** B **3.** B **4.** 542, 531, 403, 631, 325, 359, 400, 160, 179, 730, 355, 403, 655, 38, 478, 277 **5.** 289 − 285, 88 − 42 − 42, 100 − 64 − 32 **6.** 689 − 659 **7.** 549, 389, 349 **8.** (88 − 22) − 15, (175 − 67) − 39, (412 − 73) − 58 **9.** 86 + 73 = 159, 99 + 266 = 365, 96 + 178 = 274, 122 + 745 = 867, 769 + 138 = 907, 325 + 425 = 750 **10.** 120 centimeters (136 − 16 = 120) **11.** $640 (790 − 150 = 640) **12.** 218 students (247 − 29 = 218) **13.** $53 (500 − 259 − 188 = 53, or 259 + 188 = 447 and 500 − 447 = 53) **14.** $104 (128 − 6 − 6 − 6 − 6 = 104, or 6 × 4 = 24 and 128 − 24 = 104) **15.** 96 meals (213 − 117 = 96); 352 meals (1000 − 151 − 167 − 213 − 117 = 352, or 151 + 167 + 213 + 117 = 648 and 1000 − 648 = 352)

Quiz 17: Adding and Subtracting Whole Numbers

1. A **2.** B **3.** D **4.** (100 + 35) + 6, 100 + 30 + (6 + 5) **5.** 3, 4, 2, 1 **6.** 1000 − 20 − 840 − 40 = 100; 1000 − (20 + 840 + 40) = 100 **7.** 320 drinks (36 + 49 + 57 + 39 + 68 + 71 = 320); 36 drinks (36 + 49 + 57 = 142, 39 + 68 + 71 = 178, 178 − 142 = 36) **8.** 48 pages (150 − 26 − 42 − 34 = 48, or 26 + 42 + 34 = 102 and 150 − 102 = 48) **9.** Tuesday and Thursday; Monday and Wednesday; 480 sales; 6 sales; 147 sales; 134 + 134 = 268 **10.** 68 beads (18 + 18 + 24 + 8 = 68); 32 beads (100 − 68 = 32); 1 necklace and 1 anklet or 4 anklets (24 + 8 = 32, 8 + 8 + 8 + 8 = 32); 4 necklaces (100 − 4 = 96, 24 + 24 + 24 + 24 = 96)

Quiz 18: Multiplying by Multiples of 10

1. B **2.** C **3.** C **4.** 4 × 90, 6 × 60, 9 × 40 **5.** 30, 60, 90, 120, 150, 180, 210 **6.** 360 inches (9 × 40 = 360); $540 (9 × 60 = 540) **7.** 20 stickers (60 ÷ 3 = 20 or 80 ÷ 4 = 20 or 100 ÷ 5 = 20); 160 stickers (20 × 8 = 160) **8.** 80 roses (6 × 10 = 60, 2 × 10 = 20, and 60 + 20 = 80 or 6 + 2 = 8 and 8 × 10 = 80); 40 white roses (12 − 6 − 2 = 4 and 4 × 10 = 40 or 12 × 10 = 120 and 120 − 80 = 40) **9.** 20 × 9 = 180, 9 students **10.** 30 × ___ = 240, 8 markers **11.** Brynn (10 × 10 = 100 and 5 × 20 = 100); 480 points (7 + 5 + 8 + 4 = 24 and 24 × 20 = 480 or 7 × 20 + 5 × 20 + 8 × 20 + 4 × 20 = 140 + 100 + 160 + 80 = 480); Alana, Brynn, Elly, Jayda (Jayda 60 + 140 + 150 = 350, Brynn 100 + 100 + 100 = 300, Alana 40 + 160 + 50 = 250, Elly 90 + 80 + 150 = 320)

Quizzes 19 to 26: Number and Operations – Fractions

Quiz 19: Dividing into Equal Parts

1. C **2.** A **3.** $\frac{1}{8}, \frac{3}{8}$ **4.** rectangle is divided into 3 equal parts; $\frac{1}{3}$ **5.** hexagon is divided into 6 equal parts; $\frac{1}{6}$ **6.** each shape is divided into two equal halves **7.** a 3 by 6 rectangle is shaded **8.** $\frac{1}{4}, \frac{1}{4}$; The number of candies is a quarter of the total, but the total number is different so the number in a quarter is different. OR A quarter of Sam's 16 candies is 4, while a quarter of Joseph's 20 candies is 5. **9.** The shape is divided into 2 parts, but the 2 parts are not equal. **10.** 3 of the 8 equal parts are shaded; 3 of the 4 equal parts are shaded; The fraction $\frac{3}{8}$ is less than $\frac{3}{4}$ because less of the whole shape is shaded. **11.** $\frac{1}{6}, \frac{1}{6}$; The shaded area is not equal because the two whole shapes do not have equal areas.

Quiz 20: Identifying Fractions

1. A **2.** C **3.** A **4.** D **5.** C **6.** 3rd, 4th, 6th (top to bottom, left to right) **7.** $\frac{5}{6}$ **8.** B **9.** 9 of 18 squares shaded; 4 of 16 squares shaded; 5 of 15 squares shaded; 2 of 12 squares shaded; 4 of 32 squares shaded **10.** Italy, Hungary, and Chad circled; Monaco; Mauritius **11.** $\frac{1}{3}, \frac{2}{3}$

Quiz 21: Fractions and Number Lines

1. B **2.** D **3.** B **4.** $\frac{1}{4}, \frac{1}{2}$, $1\frac{1}{4}$, and $1\frac{3}{4}$ plotted **5.** number line divided into thirds, $\frac{2}{3}$ plotted **6.** $\frac{1}{8}, \frac{4}{8}, \frac{5}{8}$, and $\frac{7}{8}$ plotted; $\frac{4}{8}$ and $\frac{5}{8}$; $\frac{5}{8}$ and $\frac{7}{8}$; $\frac{4}{8}, \frac{1}{8}$ **7.** $\frac{1}{3}$, $1\frac{1}{3}$, $1\frac{2}{3}$, and $2\frac{1}{3}$ plotted; $1\frac{1}{3}$ and $2\frac{1}{3}$; 1; $1\frac{1}{3}, \frac{1}{3}$ and $1\frac{1}{3}; \frac{2}{3}$ **8.** $\frac{1}{6}, \frac{2}{6}, \frac{5}{6}$, $1\frac{3}{6}$ and $1\frac{5}{6}$ plotted on the number line; $1\frac{3}{6}$ and $1\frac{5}{6}; \frac{5}{6}, \frac{2}{6}$; $1\frac{3}{6}; \frac{2}{6}, \frac{5}{6}$ **9.** Kent Street; Maple Street; $\frac{1}{4}$ mile; $\frac{1}{2}$ mile; Butler Street **10.** the fractions plotted are $\frac{1}{2}$ or $\frac{3}{6}, \frac{2}{3}$ or $\frac{4}{6}, \frac{1}{6}$, $1\frac{1}{3}$ or $1\frac{2}{6}$, and $1\frac{5}{6}$ **11.** $\frac{1}{8}$; The race is divided into 8 equal sections, and Checkpoint A is after 1 of the 8 parts.; D; Checkpoint D is at $\frac{4}{8}$ of the race, or you can see on the number line that it is half way.

Quiz 22: Understanding Equivalent Fractions

1. $\frac{2}{6}; \frac{4}{6}; \frac{3}{6}$ **2.** 4 of 6 parts shaded; 2 of 3 parts shaded; $\frac{2}{3}$ **3.** $\frac{2}{4}, \frac{4}{8}, \frac{3}{6}$, and $\frac{1}{2}$ circled **4.** 2 of 4 parts shaded; 3 of 6 parts shaded; 4 of 8 parts shaded; $\frac{2}{4}; \frac{3}{6}; \frac{4}{8}$ **5.** 2 of 3 parts shaded; 4 of 6 parts shaded; 8 of 12 parts shaded; $\frac{4}{6}; \frac{8}{12}$ **6.** 1 of 4 parts shaded; 2 of 8 parts shaded; $\frac{2}{8}$ **7.** $\frac{2}{8} = \frac{1}{4}$ **8.** $\frac{2}{4}$ and $\frac{4}{8}, \frac{2}{8}$ and $\frac{1}{4}; \frac{6}{8}$ **9.** 1 of 2 parts shaded, 2 of 4 parts shaded, 4 of 8 parts shaded; The circles for each fraction have the same area of the circle shaded. **10.** 3 of 4 parts shaded, 6 of 8 parts shaded; The rectangles for the two fractions have the same area shaded.

Quiz 23: Generating Equivalent Fractions

1. A **2.** D **3.** B **4.** $\frac{1}{2}, \frac{3}{6}, \frac{2}{4}$ **5.** B **6.** D **7.** $\frac{1}{2}, \frac{2}{4}, \frac{3}{6}, \frac{4}{8}$ **8.** $\frac{2}{8}$ and $\frac{4}{16}$ **9.** $\frac{4}{12} = \frac{2}{6} = \frac{1}{3}$ **10.** 2 of 8 parts shaded and 4 of 16 parts shaded; $\frac{1}{4}$ **11.** 1 of 2 parts shaded, 3 of 6 parts shaded; 2 of 4 parts shaded; $\frac{2}{4}$ **12.** $\frac{2}{3}, \frac{1}{3}$; 5 plants (The student may draw a diagram or explain that there must be equal numbers of each plant for half to be parsley.) **13.** $\frac{1}{6}$ (The student may simplify $\frac{2}{12}$, use the diagram, or give a written explanation.)

Quiz 24: Whole Numbers and Fractions

1. B **2.** C **3.** D **4.** B **5.** $2\frac{3}{8}$ **6.** $\frac{30}{10}, \frac{9}{3}, \frac{6}{2}$ **7.** all fractions plotted correctly; 2, $1\frac{1}{2}, \frac{1}{2}, 1\frac{1}{3}, 1, \frac{1}{3}$ **8.** B **9.** 12 pieces **10.** $\frac{5}{2}, 2\frac{1}{2}; \frac{8}{3}, 2\frac{2}{3}; \frac{11}{8}, 1\frac{3}{8}$ **11.** $\frac{7}{2}$ or $3\frac{1}{2}$; drawing of four pairs of two triangles, 4 **12.** 3 of 8 parts shaded, $\frac{3}{8}$ **13.** diagram shaded to show two fractions that add to a whole with matching equation, such as $\frac{1}{4} + \frac{3}{4} = 1$ **14.** diagram shaded to show three fractions that add to a whole with matching equation, such as $\frac{1}{6} + \frac{2}{6} + \frac{3}{6} = 1$ **15.** diagram shaded to show three fractions that add to 2 with matching equation, such as $\frac{4}{5} + \frac{4}{5} + \frac{2}{5} = 1$

Quiz 25: Comparing Fractions

1. D **2.** B **3.** B **4.** 2, 1, 3, 4 **5.** $\frac{5}{6}, \frac{2}{3}, \frac{6}{6}, \frac{4}{6}$ **6.** A, C, E; B, D; F, G **7.** 1 of 3 equal parts shaded; 1 of 6 equal parts shaded; $\frac{1}{3} > \frac{1}{6}$ circled **8.** 3 of 4 equal parts shaded, 1 of 2 equal parts shaded, 6 of 8 equal parts shaded, 1 of 4 equal parts shaded; $\frac{3}{4}, \frac{6}{8}; \frac{1}{2}, \frac{1}{4}; \frac{1}{4}, \frac{1}{4}$ **9.** 2 of 3 equal parts shaded, 5 of 6 equal parts shaded; $\frac{2}{3}$ is less than $\frac{5}{6}$ or $\frac{5}{6}$ is greater than $\frac{2}{3}$ **10.** 7 of 10 parts shaded, 8 of 10 parts shaded; $\frac{7}{10} < \frac{4}{5}$; The student may describe how $\frac{7}{10}$ has less area shaded than $\frac{4}{5}$, or how $\frac{7}{10}$ has 7 parts shaded and $\frac{4}{5}$ has 8 parts shaded. **11.** $\frac{5}{8} > \frac{1}{2}$

Quiz 26: Using Fractions to Solve Problems

1. $\frac{1}{3}$ **2.** $\frac{1}{8}, \frac{2}{8}$ or $\frac{1}{4}$, 3 **3.** 8 serves **4.** 3 cars **5.** rectangle divided into 6 equal parts **6.** Reading; $\frac{1}{4}$; Math 30 minutes, Reading 15 minutes, Writing 45 minutes (The student may show calculations or may describe using the graph to compare the times.) **7.** Jane; $\frac{1}{6}, \frac{1}{4}, \frac{1}{2}, \frac{1}{6}$ (Jane painted 2 of 12 parts more, so $\frac{1}{6}$ more); $\frac{1}{6}$ (The student may use a diagram or give a written explanation.) **8.** $\frac{1}{3}$ (The student may use a diagram, simplify $\frac{4}{12}$, or give a written explanation.); 8 shots made, 4 shots missed (The student may use a diagram or give a written explanation.)

Quizzes 27 to 40: Measurement

Quiz 27: Writing and Measuring Time

1. B **2.** B **3.** A **4.** B **5.** 1:15, 10:30, 6:55, 6:20, 10:50, 8:45, 5:10, 12:05 **6.** 7:00, 6:00, 5:00, 11:00, 9:00 **7.** 7:25, 11:47, 10:50, 4:07, 3:26, 8:48, 12:37, 7:15

Quiz 28: Adding and Subtracting Time

1. B **2.** C **3.** D **4.** C **5.** D **6.** C **7.** 1st, 2nd, 3rd, 6th **8.** 1 hr 35 min, 1 hr 55 min, 1 hr 35 min, 2 hrs 25 min, 1 hr 40 min, 1 hr 50 min; Tim; Sonny **9.** 5:45 to 8:20; 2 hours, 35 minutes; 9:00 p.m. **10.** 3 hours, 55 minutes **11.** points plotted at 1:45 and 4:15; 2 hours, 30 minutes **12.** A at 6:00, B at 7:30, C at 7:45, D at 9:30; 3 hours, 30 minutes **13.** 1 hour 37 minutes, 9:47, 9:55, 1 hour 28 minutes, 1 hour 43 minutes, 10:01, 1 hour 49 minutes, 10:21 **14.** 6 minutes (The student may add the times to find the total time of 94 minutes, and then find that the time will be 7:34 after 94 minutes. The student may also find the time that each task ends to find the end time of 7:34.)

Quiz 29: Measuring and Estimating Liquid Volume

1. A **2.** D **3.** B **4.** 4 liters **5.** 3 liters, 20 liters, 5 liters, 35 liters **6.** lines drawn at the 75 ml mark

Quiz 30: Solving Word Problems Involving Liquid Volume

1. B **2.** B **3.** B **4.** 1 liter; 3 liters **5.** 10 liters ($5 \times 20 = 100$, $100 - 20 - 30 - 40 = 10$ or $100 - (20 + 30 + 40) = 10$) **6.** 16 loaves (Each liter can make 2, $2 \times 8 = 16$) **7.** 55 liters ($4 + 6 + 20 + 25 = 55$) **8.** line drawn at 175 ml; 175 milliliters; It is not possible because the first beaker has a volume just over 100 milliliters and cannot hold 175 milliliters. **9.** The jug and the box must have the same volume if they can hold the same amount.

Quiz 31: Measuring and Estimating Mass

1. A **2.** C **3.** A **4.** strawberry 10 grams, olive 1 gram, watermelon 1 kilogram, banana 100 grams **5.** g, kg, g, kg, kg, g **6.** 6 kilograms **7.** 4500 grams or $4\frac{1}{2}$ kilograms

Quiz 32: Solving Word Problems Involving Mass

1. D **2.** B **3.** 1st and 3rd **4.** 23 kilograms **5.** 15 kilograms ($3100 - 2800 = 300$, $300 \div 20 = 15$) **6.** 12 jars (4 lots of 3 will weigh 6 kilograms, $4 \times 3 = 12$) **7.** 49 kg; $190 ($49 - 30 = 19$, $19 \times 10 = 190$) **8.** There are more oranges than apples. 3 oranges weigh more than 2 apples, but 1 orange could weigh less than 1 apple. **9.** Jing; 4 kilograms; 1000 grams ($1500 - 500 = 1000$); 6 kilograms or 6000 grams ($1500 + 4000 + 500 = 6000$, $1\frac{1}{2} + 4 + \frac{1}{2} = 6$); Damon is correct. Damon's rocks weigh 4 kilograms. Karla and Jing's rocks weigh 2 kilograms. 4 kilograms is twice 2 kilograms.

Quiz 33: Understanding Area

1. B **2.** C **3.** 2nd and 3rd **4.** 2nd **5.** A; F; C and E; You could find the area of each banner by measuring it or tiling it. **6.** 36 square feet **7.** the rectangle is divided into 2 rows of 6 squares; 12; The area of the note paper is 12 square inches. **8.** rectangle 4 squares long and 6 squares high; rectangle 8 squares long and 5 squares high, Height = 5 cm; rectangle 9 squares long and 3 squares high, Length = 9 cm **9.** 18 square feet; The area of the large garden is 2 times the area of the small garden. 2 × 18 = 36; 6 feet (The student may draw a diagram, use an equation, or give a written explanation.)

Quiz 34: Measuring Area by Counting

1. C **2.** B **3.** 1st and 4th **4.** 6, 8, 12, 12, 16, 16 **5.** 17, 22, 20, 19, 16; C, B, E, D **6.** rectangle 6 squares long and 3 squares high; 6 × 3 = 18, 6 + 6 + 6 = 18 **7.** (3 × 2) + (7 × 2); (3 × 9) - (7 × 1) **8.** 20 square meters (The student could use an expression like (4 × 2) + (6 × 2) or could describe counting squares.); 44 square meters (The student could use an expression like (8 × 8) - 20 or could describe counting squares.) **9.** 5 square units (The student could use an expression like 15 − (2 × 5) or could describe counting squares.)

Quiz 35: Finding the Area of a Rectangle

1. D **2.** C **3.** B **4.** 32 square meters **5.** 1st, 4th, and 5th **6.** 35, 4, 3, 5, 7, 20, 3 **7.** 7 inches (7 × 8 = 56 or 56 ÷ 8 = 7) **8.** rectangles are drawn with the dimensions 4 by 6, 6 by 4, 8 by 3, and 3 by 8 **9.** 6 × 2 = 12; 4 by 3 or 3 by 4 rectangle shaded; 3 × 4 = 12 or 4 × 3 = 12 **10.** 27 square feet, 15 square feet, 12 square feet; Rectangles B and C combine to form a rectangle with the same length and height as Rectangle A. **11.** 4 squares (The student may use a diagram, an equation like 32 ÷ 8 = 4, or a written explanation.)

Quiz 36: Using Multiplication to Find Area

1. C **2.** B **3.** 1st, 4th, 6th **4.** 4 by 4 square drawn; 4 × 4 = 16 **5.** 10 and 5 or 25 and 2 (The student could use a diagram, an equation like 10 × 5 = 50, or a written explanation.); 7 feet (The student could use a diagram, an equation like 7 × 7 = 49, or a written explanation.); 22 squares (The student could use a diagram, equations like 12 × 6 = 72 and 72 − 50 = 22, or a written explanation.) **6.** 8 × 2 = 16, (4 × 2) + (4 × 2) = 16 **7.** The student could use the equations 5 × 3 = 15 and (3 × 3) + (2 × 3) = 15. The student could also use a diagram or a written explanation. **8.** 40 square inches (14 + 10 + 16 = 40); 40 ÷ 8 = 5 or 8 × ___ = 40; a 10 by 4 rectangle is drawn, 10 × 4 = 40

Quiz 37: Finding the Area of Complex Shapes

1. C **2.** B **3.** C **4.** (1 × 2) + (8 × 5), (3 × 5) + (3 × 7), (2 × 5) + (5 × 3), (3 × 8) + (4 × 3) **5.** 6 by 2 and 4 by 3 rectangle combined in any way, 5 by 2 and 3 by 3 rectangle combined in any way, 8 by 1 and 2 by 4 rectangle combined in any way **6.** 5 by 4 and 8 by 2 rectangle combined in any way; 36 square feet **7.** $111 (The student may find the area and cost for each rectangle and add them [9 × 3 = 27, 27 × 3 = 81, 2 × 5 = 10, 10 × 3 = 30, 81 + 30 =111]. The student may find the combined area and then the cost [(9 × 3) + (5 × 2) = 37, 37 × 3 = 111]) **8.** 88 square meters (The student could use the equation (10 × 4) + (6 × 8) = 88, or could show finding the area of each rectangle separately and adding them.); 192 square meters (The student could use the equation (20 × 14) - 88 = 192, or could show finding the total area and then subtracting the area of the pool.) **9.** 32 square feet (The student could use the equation 4 × 8 = 32, could count by 4s, or could give a written explanation.)

Quiz 38: Understanding and Measuring Perimeter

1. B **2.** A **3.** D **4.** 7 cm by 3 cm, 9 cm by 1 cm, 6 cm by 4 cm, 8 cm by 2 cm **5.** 4 + 3 + 2 + 4 + 2 + 7, 22 cm; 1 + 6 + 4 + 2 + 3 + 4, 20 cm; 2 + 6 + 2 + 2 + 4 + 8, 24 cm; 1 + 8 + 2 + 6 + 1 + 2, 20 cm **6.** 2 × (2 + 7) = 18, 2 + 2 + 7 + 7 = 18; 2 × (6 + 3) = 18, 6 + 6 + 3 + 3 = 18 **7.** 50 cm (6 + 13 + 3 + 4 + 15 + 9 = 50 **8.** 32 inches (The student could use the equation 8 + 8 + 8 + 8 = 32, use the diagram, or give a written explanation.) **9.** rectangle 8 squares long and 3 squares high, Perimeter = 22 cm; rectangle 10 squares long and 6 squares high, Height = 6 cm; rectangle 6 squares long and 7 squares high, Length = 6 cm **10.** Two rectangles are drawn with any of the following dimensions: 10 by 2, 9 by 3, 8 by 4, or 7 by 5. Matching perimeter equations are given, such as 2 × (10 + 2) = 24 or 9 + 3 + 9 + 3 = 24.

Quiz 39: Solving Problems Involving Perimeter

1. B **2.** C **3.** D **4.** 24 inches, 16 inches, 36 inches, 80 inches **5.** 56 cm (7 × 8 = 56 or 7 + 7 + 7 + 7 + 7 + 7 + 7 + 7 = 56); 3 cm (24 ÷ 8 = 3 or 3 + 3 + 3 + 3 + 3 + 3 + 3 + 3 = 28); 4 small boxes (4 × 24 = 96 or 24 + 24 + 24 + 24 = 96) **6.** D; B and C; A **7.** 1320 yards (100 + 120 + 100 + 120 = 440, 440 × 3 = 1320 or 440 + 440 + 440 = 1320) **8.** 8 cm (The student may use an equation like 4 + 7 + 7 + 4 + 6 + 6 + __ + __ = 50 to find the missing side, could add all the dimensions to the diagram, or could give a written explanation.) **9.** B and D have different numbers of sides. B has a perimeter of 3 + 3 + 3 = 9. D has a perimeter of 3 + 3 + 3 + 3 = 12.; A and C

Quiz 40: Relating Area and Perimeter

1. C **2.** 4, 2, 1, 3 **3.** 1st **4.** 1 and 3; 1 and 4, 2 and 3; 2 **5.** 2, 20, 16; 3, 20, 21; 4, 20, 24; 5, 20, 25 **6.** T, T, F; Lexi said that the rectangles have the same perimeter. This is incorrect because the perimeters are 18 units and 22 units. **7.** 24 square meters; 8 by 3 rectangle drawn; 7 by 3 rectangle drawn **8.** 36 square feet; 9 by 4 rectangle and 12 by 3 rectangle drawn; 6 × 6 = 36, 9 × 4 = 36, 12 × 3 = 36

Quizzes 41 to 46: Data

Quiz 41: Drawing Scaled Picture Graphs

1. circles from top to bottom: 13, 7, 9, 10, 12, 6, 5 **2.** $ from top to bottom: 9, 5, 10, 4, 7, 11, 8, 3 **3.** ✓ = 2 correct questions; ✓ from top to bottom: 7, 9, 6, 4, 10, 8, 12 **4.** ▷ = 10 pieces of pizza; triangles from top to bottom: 8, 11, 9, 6, 7, 13, 15

Quiz 42: Using Scaled Picture Graphs to Solve Problems

1. 6 emails; 4 emails; Monday; Monday and Tuesday; Thursday and Monday; 48 emails **2.** 40 minutes; Tuesday; 40 minutes; 100 minutes; Thursday and Friday; 250 minutes **3.** 45 + 30 = 75, 75 votes; 60 – 20 = 40, 40 votes; 25 + 15 = 40, 40 votes; 40 – 15 = 25, 25 votes **4.** 10 pennies (55 – 45 = 10); 15 pennies (50 – 35 = 15); 105 pennies (40 + 65 = 105)

Quiz 43: Drawing Scaled Bar Graphs

1. all bars drawn to correct heights. **2.** scale in units of 15, all bars drawn to correct heights **3.** scale in units of 5, all bars drawn to correct heights **4.** horizontal axis is labeled "Color" with the colors listed, vertical axis is labeled "Number of Votes" with a scale in units of 2, all bars drawn to correct heights

Quiz 44: Using Scaled Bar Graphs to Solve Problems

1. 30; pumpkin; cherry; cherry and pecan; 80; blueberry; peach and pecan; $90 **2.** 8; Jin; Isaac and Adam; 32; Andre; 4; 16; Isaac and Jin, Andre and Tom **3.** 40 + 55 = 95, 95 minutes; 45 – 25 = 20, 20 minutes; 50 - 20 = 30, 30 minutes; 25 + 45 + 30 = 100, 100 minutes **4.** 14 – 7 = 7, 7 cars; 22 + 17 + 20 = 59, 59 cars; Jamie is correct. There are 22 white cars. There are 13 + 7 = 20 blue and yellow cars combined. **5.** True, 3, 6; False, 14, 9, 5; True, 15, 17; False, 11, 3, 14 **6.** 20 bookmarks (40 – 20 = 20); 25 bookmarks (45 – 20 = 25); 180 bookmarks (35 + 15 + 40 + 20 + 25 + 45 = 180)

Quiz 45: Measuring Length

1. C **2.** C **3.** 6 inches **4.** $3\frac{1}{4}$ inches **5.** $4\frac{1}{2}$, $3\frac{1}{2}$, $2\frac{1}{2}$, 2 **6.** $4\frac{1}{4}$, $5\frac{1}{2}$, $1\frac{1}{4}$ **7.** total of 7 bricks $1\frac{1}{2}$ inches long; $10\frac{1}{2}$ inches **8.** $7\frac{1}{2}$ inches; rectangle divided into three parts $2\frac{1}{2}$ inches long; $2\frac{1}{2}$ inches **9.** $2\frac{1}{4}$, $1\frac{3}{4}$, 2, $1\frac{1}{2}$, 1, $1\frac{1}{4}$; $1\frac{1}{4}$ inches ($2\frac{1}{4}$ – 1 = $1\frac{1}{4}$, or the student may describe using the rulers to count the difference.) **10.** rectangle drawn for Margo $3\frac{3}{4}$ inches long, rectangle drawn for Pierre 5 inches long; Chang $4\frac{1}{2}$ inches, Margo $3\frac{3}{4}$ inches, Pierre 5 inches

Quiz 46: Representing Length on Line Plots

1. B **2.** points plotted as follows: 4 points for $6\frac{1}{2}$, 3 points for 7, 3 points for $7\frac{1}{2}$, 4 points for 8, 2 points for $8\frac{1}{2}$ **3.** points plotted as follows: 1 point for $4\frac{1}{4}$, 2 points for $4\frac{1}{2}$, 4 points for $4\frac{3}{4}$, 1 point for 5, 1 point for $5\frac{1}{2}$ **4.** points plotted as follows: 3 points for $1\frac{3}{4}$, 1 point for 2, 3 points for $2\frac{1}{4}$, 3 points for $2\frac{1}{2}$, 2 points for $2\frac{3}{4}$; 9 plants; The student should describe counting the number of points for 2 or more. **5.** $2\frac{3}{4}$, $3\frac{3}{4}$, 3, $3\frac{3}{4}$, 3, 3, $3\frac{1}{2}$, $2\frac{1}{4}$; points plotted as follows: 1 point for $2\frac{1}{4}$, 1 point for $2\frac{3}{4}$, 3 points for 3, 1 point for $3\frac{1}{2}$, 2 points for $3\frac{3}{4}$; 3 inches; The student should describe how you can compare how many points are plotted for each length.

Quizzes 47 to 52: Geometry

Quiz 47: Understanding the Properties of Shapes

1. A **2.** C **3.** 1st, 4th, 5th **4.** trapezoid; triangle and pentagon **5.** A, D, F, G; B, C, E, H; 5, 6
6. pentagon drawn; 5; 5; pentagon **7.** Annabelle is not correct because parallelograms have two pairs of parallel sides, and the trapezoid only has 1 pair. **8.** 1st, 3rd, 4th; square with side lengths of 4 units, rectangle with a height twice its width, trapezoid with a right angle and parallel sides 2 and 5 units long **9.** All the shapes have at least 1 right angle.; The first two shapes have 4 sides or are quadrilaterals. The last shape has 3 sides, or is a triangle.

Quiz 48: Comparing Shapes

1. C **2.** 3, 4, 2, 1 **3.** B **4.** D; A; B; C and D **5.** 4, 4; 4, 4; 4 or all, 4 or all; 2 pairs, 2 pairs; 4; 2 pairs; whether a shape has 4 equal sides or 2 pairs of equal sides **6.** Any three of the four similarities: They both have four sides. They both have equal side lengths. They both have 4 angles. They both have two pairs of parallel sides.; Squares have 4 equal angles. Squares have right angles. **7.** They are both quadrilaterals, both have 4 sides, or are both trapezoids.; The second shape has a right angle or does not have two sides with the same length. **8.** any 4-sided shape drawn; any 3-sided shape drawn **9.** a 4-sided shape with no equal side lengths; any 7-sided shape; any 6-sided shape; a 5-sided shape with no equal side lengths

Quiz 49: Classifying Shapes

1. B **2.** A **3.** D **4.** B **5.** C **6.** square, rhombus, rectangle **7.** (left to right, top to bottom) 2nd, 6th, 8th; All the octagons have 8 sides or 8 angles. **8.** square and triangle; rectangle and triangle; hexagon and rectangle; pentagon and rectangle; pentagon and triangle; hexagon and triangle **9.** C; 4 sides, equal side lengths, 2 pairs of parallel sides; A; 4 sides, a pair of parallel sides; F; 4 equal sides, 4 right angles

Quiz 50: Identifying and Drawing Quadrilaterals

1. B **2.** 2nd, 3rd, 6th **3.** square and rhombus drawn; square, rhombus **4.** 1 square, 1 parallelogram, 5 triangles; 1 square, 2 parallelograms, 3 triangles; 1 rectangle, 1 square, 1 parallelogram, 5 triangles; 1 square, 2 parallelograms, 3 triangles **5.** (left to right, top to bottom) 2nd, 6th, 8th, 10th; rhombus and rectangle; drawing of a square, square **6.** drawing of a 4 by 8 rectangle, rectangle; any trapezoid with a right angle, trapezoid; any rhombus, rhombus; square with side lengths of 5 units, square

Quiz 51: Dividing Shapes into Equal Parts

1. B **2.** D **3.** A **4.** 1st, 3rd, 4th **5.** each shape is divided into two equal triangles **6.** second circle divided into equal quarters, third circle divided into equal sixths, third circle divided into equal eighths **7.** rectangle divided into equal quarters, rectangle divided into equal sixths, rectangle divided into equal eighths **8.** divided into three 2 by 7 rectangles; divided into three 1 by 8 rectangles; divided into three 3 by 8 rectangles

Quiz 52: Using Shapes to Understand Fractions

1. B **2.** C **3.** D **4.** 6 pieces **5.** divided into equal halves, $\frac{1}{2}$ shaded; divided into equal quarters, $\frac{1}{4}$ shaded; divided into equal sixths, $\frac{1}{6}$ shaded; divided into equal fifths, $\frac{1}{5}$ shaded; divided into equal thirds, $\frac{1}{3}$ shaded **6.** Danny; 2, 1; 3, 4; Kasim **7.** Julie; Dana shaded 2 parts instead of 1. Emiko did not divide the rectangle into equal parts. Tiana divided the rectangle into 8 parts instead of 4. **8.** $\frac{1}{8}$ **9.** circle divided into equal thirds; Kate's circle has 3 parts, but they are not equal. The circle I divided has 3 equal parts. **10.** 8 by 2 rectangle shaded

Get to Know Our Product Range

Mathematics

Practice Test Books
Practice sets and practice tests will prepare students for the state tests.

Common Core Quiz Books
Focused individual quizzes cover every math skill one by one.

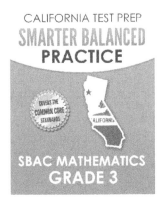 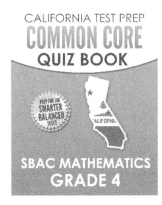 

English Language Arts/Reading

Practice Test Books
Practice sets and practice tests will prepare students for the state tests.

Reading Skills Workbooks
Short passages and question sets will develop and improve reading comprehension skills and are perfect for ongoing test prep.

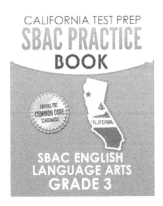 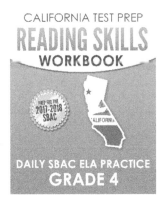 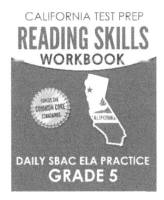

Writing

Writing Skills Workbooks
Students write narratives, essays, and opinion pieces, and write in response to passages.

Persuasive and Narrative Writing Workbooks
Guided workbooks teach all the skills needed to write narratives and opinion pieces.

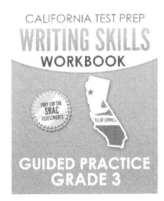 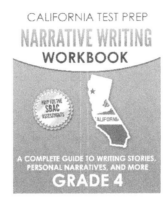 

Language and Vocabulary

Language and Vocabulary Quiz Books
Focused quizzes cover spelling, grammar, usage, writing conventions, and vocabulary.

Revising and Editing Workbooks
Students improve language skills and writing skills by identifying and correcting errors.

Language Skills Workbooks
Exercises on specific language skills including figurative language, synonyms, and homographs.

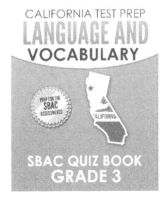 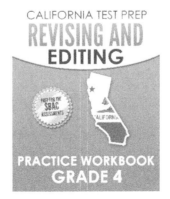 

http://www.testmasterpress.com

Made in the USA
Las Vegas, NV
10 March 2025

19347762R10129